A Family Meeting Handbook:

Achieving Family Harmony Happily

by

Robert Slagle, Ph.D.

A Family Meeting Handbook:

Achieving Family Harmony Happily

by

Robert Slagle, Ph.D.

Family Relations Foundation

The characters in the cover illustration were modeled after a drawing by a six-year-old client who was depicting members of her family as they were about to hold their first Family Meeting.

TO ORDER copies of **A Family Meeting Handbook** from the publisher, please refer to final page of the text.

Published by: **Family Relations Foundation, Inc.**
P.O. Box 462
Sebastopol, California 95472 U.S.A.

Illustrations and cover design: Robert W. Slagle

Typography by: Vera Allen Composition, Castro Valley, CA.

International Standard Book Number 0-9614218-0-0

Library of Congress Catalog Card Number 84-82425

Library of Congress Cataloging in Publication Data

Slagle, Robert W. (Robert William), 1942-
A family meeting handbook.

Bibliography: p. 145
1. Family. 2. Meetings. 3. Parenting. I. Title.
HQ734.S666 1985 646.7′8 84-82425
ISBN 0-9614218-0-0 (pbk.)

First Edition
1 2 3 4 5 6 7 8 9

Printed in the United States of America

Foreword

This handbook is based on personal experience. I first became intrigued with the idea of Family Meetings when I was introduced to a family that held them. I was not impressed at first, but one aspect of this family's procedure stuck in my mind. Although there were seven children in the family, the father reported that family disturbances were rare. *What amazed me was the fact that the children were never punished unless they willingly agreed to the punishment.* The extraordinary fairness of this rule, along with my curiosity about how it could possibly work effectively, hooked me. In my own home, we began experimenting with Family Meetings when our two boys were about five and seven years old. Our focus was on fairness, "listening," and cooperation for the benefit of the family as a whole. After we established precedents and trust in the process, our meetings became easier. Before long, I began to wonder why more parents did not use Family Meetings. In our home, the effects of Family Meetings were unquestionably positive and successful.

I introduced the procedure into my family counseling practice. This was a rigorous testing, since most families that come to me for therapeutic intervention are in a crisis. A teenage girl has been arrested for alcohol and drug possession. A ten-year-old boy has become so hyperactive that he cannot be retained in school. What should a family do in cases such as these? Making Family Meetings successful is a relatively long-term venture. Family Meetings would seem difficult to apply in a crisis situation when there has been no preparation for the procedure. Yet, even under these trying situations, Family Meetings proved invaluable. In my service as a Marriage Counselor and Family Therapist, I have not seen even one problem that could not be handled by Family Meetings as described in this handbook. I have, in good conscience, been able to guarantee parents powerful benefits from Family Meetings when the procedure is given a fair chance.

Explaining the details of the process to families eventually became so time-consuming that I wrote a brief guide—essentially the first portion of this handbook. Year after year, parents asked for more detailed information, and I longed to expand the brief paper into a manual or handbook. Over fifteen years of Family Meetings involving scores of families have assured and reassured me of the fundamental transformative power of Family Meetings. *Such transformations can be observed within three to six months provided there is sincere intent and meetings are held regularly.*

The idea of Family Meetings must be obvious and not particularly exciting to some parents. It is easy to overlook the rich harvests from Family Meetings because the idea is so deceptively simple. Some parents dismiss family council practices with faint praise. "Oh, we've done that for years at the supper table." When I probe further, almost invariably I find that the "meetings" are quite different in principle than those depicted in this manual. Based on my experience, the "rules" and suggestions expressed here work; and, they are flexible enough to be adapted to the uniqueness of your family. I welcome your letters, comments, inquiries, and anecdotes. (Please see the final page of this handbook.)

After completing this writing, I surveyed some of the literature that pertains to family council practices. Dodson's system of fathering, Gordon's P.E.T. "method III" system, and the philosophy of Dreikurs are compatible with the Family Meeting process as I know it. I have added to the text an annotated bibliography that I believe will enrich and embellish your Family Meeting efforts.

I am truly grateful to the many families who inspired this handbook and to those families who granted permission to tell some of their Family Meeting episodes. For editorial, design, and technical assistance, I want to thank Mary Mitchell, Bob Hunt, Brian Erwin, Laura Nixon, Carol Kristensen, and Sandy Goodwin. In particular I want to extend my appreciation to Chris and Alex Rood, Elizabeth van Buren, Geri Olson, Olga Senyk, Cheryl and Dick Prince, Bonnie and Bob Hunt, Barbara and Sam La Rue, and Doris Meunier for their loving support.

R. S.

CONTENTS

FAMILY MEETINGS

Introduction

Please consider how many overworked fathers there are who spend too little time with their children and feel guilty as a result. A father's scarce time is often spent dealing with the children *as problems* with little or no time just for fun. Consider how many mothers find themselves short on patience and long on guilt, worried and worn from cycles of their children "acting up," with yelling and snarled emotions sometimes lingering for days. Yet these mothers and fathers are usually concerned parents who want the best for their children. For Mom, some days seem wasted on unrewarding pursuits, nagging questions, sibling quarrels, or injured feelings. At the end of a day all Mom wants is "out." To make matters worse, the next day and the next are likely to be the same wearisome routine. Each of many issues demands a great deal of parental energy, and there still seems to be no "good time" with the kids. Both parents are exhausted and may wish the children would simply go away. So, the kids "act up" again and force parental attention; but, as usual, it is negative attention. Before long both parents are resenting their youngsters and are finding ways to shut them out.

This is hardly a beautiful vision of family harmony. The absurd thing is that the actual amount of time these parents spend dealing with their children is already more than what is needed for successful Family Meetings and their associated family activities. Why not take the easy way out with your family? Read this manual thoroughly, take Family Meetings seriously, acknowledge that you will have to make a time commitment for several months and utilize one or two hours of your prime time each week. This is a modest price when you consider the alternative of spending an equivalent amount of time each week having to discipline your children. Even if your job as parent is relatively easy sailing right now, Family Meetings will only make it better and provide you with valuable insurance against troubled waters that may arise in later years. Family Meetings can provide relief and flexibility so that if, because of work or other circumstances, you feel unable to spend a lot of time with your kids, you do not have to. The family can still function smoothly. Family Meetings make the hardest things for parents easier: not getting angry, being patient, and being consistent. If you hunger for more "quality" time with your children, you will have it. What could be better?

* * *

Consider the following two family dramas.

Scene: At home, school night, 9:00 p.m., Mom (*age 27*), Dad (*age 31*), Jimmy (*age 6*), Robert (*age 9*)

Drama A.

"Robert and Jimmy . . . ! (*pause*) Jimmy! Robert! Do you know what time it is? (*silence*) Are you ready for bed?"

"No."

"Have you cleaned up your room and brushed your teeth?"

"No."

(Mom *and* Dad *go into boys' room, toys and papers all over the floor.*) "Do you guys know what time it is? How many times have we told you . . .!?"

Drama B.

"Mom, Dad, we're ready to say good night." (Mom *and* Dad *both go to the door, lights are out, both boys in their beds waiting for a good night kiss.*)

"Did you guys brush your teeth and clean up?"

"Yes."

"Yes."

"Good night boys, sleep well."

If scenes like **A** are all too familiar in your household, Family Meetings are a sure way to transform those repetitive daily tussles into matter-of-fact, even joyful, interactions. If the scene in **B** is more like your home life, Family Meetings can only further enhance an already good situation. Drama **B** is taken from the same family as in drama **A** after ten months of Family Meetings.

Beginning Your Own Family Meetings

Family Meetings are a sure way of bettering family relationships, solving problems, and above all, nurturing opportunities for children to learn fairness, respect, and self-esteem. ***The key principle of Family Meetings is that family decisions are made by everyone's agreement.*** Because of this it is important to include all the children and parents or all the people living under the same roof. Family Meetings may be times of praise for good behavior and deciding consequences for objectionable behavior. They are times for giving out allowances or rewards, for planning family events, for planning the week's activities, for playing games, for reading or working together. Family Meetings should provide for discussion of whatever anyone in the family wants to bring up.

The first step is for the parents to make a commitment to follow through with some stated minimum number of meetings (at least ten or twelve) regardless of the apparent short-term outcome. Next, the parents should get together and discuss the procedure and plan the strategy for their first Family Meeting. They should agree ahead of time as to the topics and issues that will be included in the Family Meetings. Not every family issue is appropriate for the Family Meeting since some of the children may not be mature enough to be involved in certain decisions (for example, financial ones) which do not directly affect them. However, Family Meetings should include all of those issues that actually affect the children, who in turn affect the well-being and harmony of the entire family.

Suggested topics for your first Family Meeting:

1) **The rules of Family Meetings.**—Make sure everyone understands the meaning of the word "concensus." A Family Meeting decision is only valid if every family member voluntarily agrees to it. Otherwise, you must either persuade (not force) some voters to change their minds, or else you must compromise to win everyone's vote.

2) **Sharing responsibilities around the home.**—The meeting leader should ask each family member what duties she or he agrees to perform each week. The fairness of these duties to the persons involved should be discussed. Don't tackle too much at once. If each person agrees to just one or two duties, that is a good start for your first Family Meeting.

3) **Consequences.**—Build into every family agreement the consequence for failing to keep that agreement. Rather than thinking of a "consequence" as negative, it can be viewed as a natural and worthwhile means of learning how to keep agreements.

4) **Parents' rights and authority.**—At the first or second Family Meeting parents can ask for a family agreement about what Mom or Dad can require of a child without having a Family Meeting to decide that requirement. For instance, many families decide that either parent can send a child to his or her room to think a good thought without having a special Family Meeting to determine the fairness of that discipline. Deep down, children usually respect their parents' authority and want to be obedient, so long as the youngster understands the purpose of what is being asked of him.

5) **Family activities.**—Remember to keep your meetings light-hearted and brief. Don't try to include too many topics or handle too much discipline. Be wise in assessing the limits of your family's first meeting. A family outing or game right after this first meeting

will be an important bonus for your efforts. After you decide on your family activity, remember to agree on the time and place of the next meeting, and remember to write down your family decisions in your Family Meeting notebook.

It is tremendously important that Family Meetings be held regularly, preferably once a week, and that they be held at a time when everybody is relatively fresh, alert, and awake. Sunday is often a good day for Family Meetings since everyone is usually more or less rested and able to be attentive for these few minutes. It is likely to prove unsuccessful to meet at a time when everyone is especially tired from work, play, or school.

Family Meetings should be kept short—not ordinarily longer than an hour or an hour and a half, and preferably as brief as thirty minutes. The right amount of time for your family can be judged by observing the attention span of the younger children. For children under seven, for instance, Family Meetings that extend beyond 20 or 30 minutes will wind down as the children become restless and inattentive. For older children and teenagers, Family Meetings may extend to an hour, but beyond this time it is usually better to delay further business until the next meeting.

It is critically important that Family Meetings have a positive association for the children, and, of course, for parents as well. In other words, the Family Meeting should not be simply a court for discipline, but should be the time and place when problems are discussed, plans are made, and when each child has an opportunity to speak openly regarding his or her own needs and desires. It is also extremely important that Family Meetings be a time of praise and reward for jobs well done, achievements, positive attitude, and progress by any family member, including a parent.

The Story of One Family's First Meeting

Here is an example of a Family Meeting to illustrate how it works and some of its uses:

Don (*Dad, age 32*), Julie (*Mom, age 31*),
Nancy (*age 11*), Robert (*age 8*), and Jimmy (*age 4*)

Julie and Don agreed ahead of time on the strategy of guiding Family Meetings to include decisions regarding tasks and jobs each family member should be responsible for during the week. Daily responsibilities might include getting up on time in the morning, getting dressed, making their beds, emptying the garbage, and getting to bed on time in the evening. Julie and Don also decided that problems that involved themselves exclusively, and not the children, would not be included in Family Meetings. However, they did recognize that the children should be allowed every opportunity to express their views and to acquire fairness within the family structure. Of course, Don and Julie's strategy regarding their Family Meetings had to be agreed upon voluntarily by the kids as the process unfolded.

Initially, Julie and Don spoke to their children one-to-one, describing how Family Meetings would help each child to feel better, to enjoy the family more, and to earn those things each youngster desires. Also, the children were given an explanation of how Family Meetings work for their good, provide fairness and allow more opportunities to voice their opinions than they would get from just speaking to one or the other parent. Next, Julie and Don asked the children if they would agree to try Family Meetings. The two older children agreed readily, but little Jimmy was not sure. With a little encouraging, he agreed to try once. Julie and Don suggested Sunday noon as the time of their meetings, since this was a time when they all were relatively refreshed and free from other commitments. The children agreed.

Before lunch on Sunday, Julie called the children together and asked everyone to come to the Family Meeting. It took a few minutes and a little effort to focus everyone's energy, but finally everyone was sitting around the kitchen table ready to begin. They decided that for each meeting a different person would write down the minutes of the meeting in a notebook. Nancy volunteered to be the note-taker for the first meeting. She wrote down the date and indicated that everyone was present at the meeting. Although Jimmy was too young to take notes or to be entirely involved in all the decisions at the meeting, he was encouraged to draw the cover for their Family Meeting notebook.

Since it is up to parents to keep the focus of attention on the particular issue at hand, Julie (Mom) began the first meeting by asking Robert what he thought his work around the house should be. All the children were given a little time to think about what their *fair* contribution to the family's activities might be. The older children made notes and listed the chores and duties they thought they should do. Don (Dad) asked Robert if he had thought of things that would be fair duties for him to perform and also what reward or allowance he should receive each week for properly doing his share. After a couple of interruptions from Jimmy and a little fidgeting on Robert's part, Robert suggested that he ought to make his own bed, get dressed in the mornings, brush his teeth at night, and go to bed by nine without being asked or reminded. Robert also agreed that he should clean out the doghouse, feed the fish, and water the flowers in the backyard every other day. He thought he should get a dollar a week for his share of the family work. Don and Julie both mentioned to Robert that a dollar was quite a bit for the chores he agreed to and perhaps it would be fair if he got a little less.

With the focus always on arriving at what is fair, the conclusion was finally reached between Robert, Don and Julie that sixty-five cents each week would be a fair amount. Next, Julie asked each of the other children, "Do you think it's fair that your brother gets sixty-five cents for doing these household activities?" Jimmy was not sure. He had been a bit distracted, but when Don and Julie explained to Jimmy that he would have his turn, too, and would receive an amount that was fair to him, he agreed, as did Nancy. Robert's allowance and duties were specified for the week and written down in the weekly notebook.

After a little talk and coaxing, everyone agreed that Jimmy would help Mom set the table at night and do a few other daily chores. Since Jimmy was too young to fully understand the meaning of money, everyone agreed that he would receive ten marbles each week if he did his duties properly. Next, Nancy got her turn. After some discussion, she worked out her duties and allowance, and won everyone's agreement. Finally, Julie and Don each had a turn to describe some of the things they do, how mothers and fathers are rewarded, and how the children could help them and reward them by cooperating.

Julie was somewhat anxious to get to the matter of discipline, since Robert had been rather rowdy at school and had even provoked the necessity of a teacher conference. Ordinarily Robert had been spanked for his rowdy behavior, but in the last year or so this had seemed less and less effective. During this meeting, Robert was asked what he thought would be fair discipline for either his mother or father to give to him if they caught him doing something they regarded as wrong or "out-of-line." Good and fair consequences proved difficult to find, but finally Robert agreed that any time his parents thought he was doing something wrong, they could, at their discretion, ask him to go to his room for ten minutes. During this time, he was to think of some good thing that he had done or heard or been involved with that day. He would then report this to his parent(s). When either Julie or Don was satisfied that Robert had actually thought a good thought, he was to be permitted to go back to business as usual. Everyone, including Robert, agreed upon this procedure.

After more discussion, the whole family decided that no punishment would be given out by the parents, other than asking a child to go to his or her room and think a good thought. Any other discipline or punishment must be given by way of the Family Meeting, with each person, even the offending child, agreeing freely to the fairness of that punishment. By this time, Jimmy was getting restless. Even Don was a little agitated, because he was weary from concentrating on keeping the ball rolling and keeping everyone's attention on what just one person was saying. At this point, Julie suggested that they end the Family Meeting for this week and continue on the fol-

lowing Sunday. At Julie's suggestion, they closed the family meeting with everyone holding hands and singing a little song that Robert had just learned at school.

Ten Ingredients for Successful Family Meetings

One family's style with Family Meetings may be surprisingly different from that of any other family. Meeting agendas will vary from family to family as will types of rewards and consequences used. There does seem to be a common denominator of ingredients found in successful Family Meetings. These ingredients are typical of, if not essential to, maximizing the effectiveness and minimizing the effortfulness of Family Meetings. Here are ten valuable ingredients.

1) **Consensus.**—A family decision is made only if every single member of the family voluntarily agrees to it.

2) **Willingness.**—There must be openness and willingness to abide by the Family Meeting rules and decisions. Parents, especially, must be willing to trust the process!

3) **Patience.**—The major reason Family Meetings may appear to be unsuccessful at first is that parents become impatient and give up prematurely. The results attainable within a few months or a dozen or so meetings are well worth the wait.

4) **One hour per week, or less, of prime time.**—It is a small but invaluable amount of your total week. Family Meetings usually take less than an hour and rarely more. It is critical, however, that your family picks a time that is "good" or "prime time," a time when the children are reasonably rested and everyone more or less has their wits about them.

5) **A pleasant and private setting.**—The kitchen, living room, or bedroom is fine, so long as everyone can be attentive. Plan your setting so as to minimize the likelihood of interruption. This may require turning off the phone, putting a "Do Not Disturb" note on the door, informing friends of your regular meeting time, and otherwise doing whatever it takes to insure the priority of your Family Meeting session.

6) **Participation.**—The entire family should be present for each meeting. Since consensus requires everyone's agreement, a valid family decision needs the support of every voter. If a member of your family is going to miss one or more meetings, his or her vote can be transferred to another family member (if everyone agrees). Be sure your family has regular Family Meetings with everyone attending at least often enough to maintain the continuity of the process. Attempt to work out a reasonable agreement about attendance that everyone can follow. In fact, there is no reason why attendance cannot be tangibly rewarded. The Family Meeting is that important!

7) **A notebook.**—You should have and maintain a Family Meeting log book or journal in which you keep the minutes of every Family Meeting. A large spiral or loose leaf binder or a blank bound journal will serve this purpose. Why not choose an attractive journal at the outset to underscore the importance of your undertaking?

8) **Friendly feelings.**—Initiating a Family Meeting when you are in a huff, a miff, or a snit is a prescription for failure. Plan ahead and prepare a time when you are reasonably sure that everyone can handle a meeting with at least a hint of good cheer. One of the great advantages of Family Meetings is that decisions are made dispassionately, objectively, and thought-

fully. If you can't have a Family Meeting with reasonably good feelings, don't have it.

9) **Spiritual faith.**—Family Meetings can be an opportunity for meditation and worship, but they need not be. However, if Family Meetings are seen in the context of a greater power or higher values, it's like adding sails to your ship.

10) **More patience.**—It's like planting seeds and waiting for the harvest. There's just no way to hurry the process. Even if you've had regular Family Meetings for weeks with little noticeable improvements in conduct or family harmony, your effort toward Family Meetings is always time well spent. Hang in there. Your seeds will sprout.

Understanding the Family Meeting Process

Not only do Family Meetings bring direct and often dramatic improvements in family relations, but also these benefits are amazingly substantial and enduring. Sometimes meetings are difficult at first, requiring a lot of patience and tenacity. Over time, Family Meetings prove themselves again and again. The easing of pressures during other times of the week makes the weekly meetings well worthwhile. They will pay off many fold over the years to come. It is very natural to have resistance to Family Meetings, and at some time or another each and every person may resist coming to the meeting for one reason or another. If this is the case, try to shorten the meeting and allow time for some positive and enjoyable activity—such as playing a game that everyone likes—in order to keep the meeting on a positive note. Once in a while, Family Meetings will seem to fall short of the expectations parents have. Even if the meetings are cut short or aborted before all of the business is complete, they will, after the weeks go by, prove to be more and more fruitful. Even the children will enjoy coming to them because they learn gradually that this is a place where they can be heard, where they are listened to, and where they have an equal and powerful vote in everything that is decided. It's a thrill when after weeks of effort your children come to remind you that it is time for a Family Meeting and do so with no prompting on your part.

Again and again, the key process is consensus: every decision is made by the freewill agreement of each and every person. It is not possible for three out of five family members to outvote the other two. It may seem impossible to reach a consensus on many decisions. Consensus allows anyone, even the youngest child, the option of boycotting or filibustering a Family Meeting. In practice, this does not happen for long. The great power of each vote proves not to be a weakness but a strength to the

Family Meeting process. Children learn that they cannot block the process indefinitely and still have their own needs met. The built-in checks and balances of consensual decision-making in a small group are so strong that speedy consensus can usually be reached even when it means a child votes for his own disciplinary consequence.

Family Meetings take away the option of arbitrary punishment by either parent such as spanking a child on the spur of the moment when he or she has provoked the parent or done something exceedingly wrong. Some parents feel limited by the seeming fact that they cannot act on their own authority to discipline their children on the spot. There simply is no such limit. If the violation is truly severe, a special Family Meeting can be held immediately. Usually children will agree by consensus to allow their parents reasonable disciplinary discretion on the spur of the moment. Most children crave their guardians to set limits and consequences on their conduct. A context of permissiveness usually results in an insecure if not a "spoiled" child. It is a parent's right and duty to negotiate within a meeting for whatever parental prerogatives and authority can be agreed upon by all. Otherwise, discipline should be deferred until the next regular Family Meeting, there to be taken up and agreed upon by everybody in the fairest way possible.

At each Family Meeting, once a congenial tone is established, the business of "follow-up" from the last meeting is begun. The notes from the previous Family Meeting are reviewed to see what issues are to be taken up or if some lagging matter is to be a part of the present meeting. Each child gets a turn to share what he or she has done during the week to earn his or her allowance. Each child tells of his or her activities and is then asked what he or she thinks is a fair amount of allowance or reward. Negotiation begins and finally amounts are agreed upon by everyone.

It works best if consequences can be agreed upon ahead of time. For example, in the "Story of One Family's First Family Meeting," suppose that Robert has agreed that if he doesn't go to bed on time without being asked, he will be charged a nickel for each night he fails. If, after several weeks, this does not work, the Family Meeting is used to find a different consequence, one that may work better to assist Robert to change his behavior.

Paramount among consequences are praise and reward. For instance, in a subsequent Family Meeting, Nancy does her week of work exceptionally well, and both Julie and Don praise her highly. After some discussion, it is agreed that the whole family will go horseback

riding, as this is something Nancy has wanted to do for many months. It cannot be overemphasized how important immediate praise and reward are for supporting and acknowledging good behavior and a good attitude. For each child, attention is first drawn to what they did well, how they succeeded, what they achieved. They are praised for their accomplishments or given additional allowance for jobs well done where monetary reward is appropriate. In fact, over time, praise and reward alone will wipe out most undesirable behavior. The praised and rewarded activities will come to dominate, and eventually there will simply be no time or energy left for the inappropriate or upsetting conduct. In Family Meetings, children quickly learn self-imposed responsibility, taking accountability for their own doings. This relieves parents on a day-to-day basis and engenders a sense of family unity and mutual devotion.

Ever so gradually, meeting by meeting, the children will earn self-respect and accept as fact that a Family Meeting is their best opportunity to receive fairness regarding their own needs and wishes. The children eventually begin to recognize that their voices are heard and that they have rights, too, albeit not the same rights as their parents or even the older children. Kids learn that they will not be visited with arbitrary punishment, yet they cannot get away with wrongdoing since all these matters are sooner or later brought up at the Family Meeting or reviewed from the notes from previous meetings. ***Remember: Postponement need not be avoidance.*** One of the great values of Family Meetings is that they drastically cut down on the weekly or daily harangues that go on within a family, especially those one-to-one conflicts where no problem-solving really takes place but only hurt feelings and upset emotions get more or less ventilated.

Family Meetings rest on the assumption that children are naturally positive in their attitudes. They have to learn to be negative. It's surprising what children will willingly agree to in a Family Meeting when their minds are approached with love and common sense. It's valuable in one of the early meetings to establish (by consensus) the ground rules for parents' authority. What are the rights that parents should have without calling a special meeting? Parents occasionally feel that by giving up their sovereignty to the supersovereignty of the family as a whole, they are somehow losing power. Not so. Parents actually gain, not lose, personal power in relation to their children. Meanwhile, children gain a gradual sense that their parents' power will be levied even more fairly than before they began Family Meetings. Disciplinary precedents should be set early and adhered to consistently. It works!

If the overall results of Family Meetings were not well worth the effort, no family would have them. Yet, the number of families having meetings is growing rapidly, and there are numerous anecdotes acclaiming their value. The first few weeks or even months of Family Meetings are sometimes slow and frustrating and may seem a total failure. Do not be fooled by appearances. Just getting together with the intention of having a meeting each week will have beneficial effects, even if no apparent progress in the children's growth or behavior is noticed.

If a participant in your Family Meeting becomes overly emotional during the session, it may be wise to cut the meeting short, table the issue, and take it all up again when everyone is rested and more cheerful. For a while, a family may complain that Family Meetings are only a series of tabled and emotionally freighted issues that never get dealt with. Nevertheless, press on. Recall that meetings are not meant primarily to be a courtroom. Sometimes it is best to wipe the slate clean regarding consequences for an offending child and to reestablish the meeting experience as positive and nurturing. Go to the beach, have a picnic, take in a movie in place of making the Family Meeting the source of constant punishment. Children must perceive the weekly meeting as a place to obtain fairness in grievances and to have more, not less, of their personal needs and wants met. In Family Meetings, everybody works for everybody. Everyone wins.

Benefits of Family Meetings

Belonging. Even though children automatically "belong" to some kind of a family, having regular Family Meetings greatly heightens a youngster's sense of belonging and of being an important part of a well defined group—the family.

Self-esteem. Because Family Meetings involve making decisions by consensus, each child quickly acquires a sense of his own unique importance in the group. Each youngster's vote is needed and is essential to the process. In Family Meetings a child's self-worth is not based on age, accomplishments, or popularity, but on decision power. A child has the same voting power regardless of his or her physical size, age, or success in other situations.

Earning your own way. What we commonly call "spoiling" a child usually has to do with the youngster receiving unearned rights, privileges, and gifts. So-called "spoiled" children usually encounter difficulty out in the "real world" because very few things come free. Also, the youngster has not learned the relative value of things. Family Meetings diminish the usual sense of powerlessness children feel and grant them a sense of confidence—power to earn, to work for worthwhile attainables. In Family Meetings, statements like, "You can't have that," or "Wait until you're older" are typically transformed into the question, "What will it take to earn that?"

Share and compromise. Although the benefits of Family Meetings often come at a snail's pace, demanding much patience, children gradually learn that you don't always get what you want unless you are willing to cooperate with other members of the family. "Give and take" is not so much a rule of the meetings as an inevitability.

Reaping what you sow. Through Family Meetings, children get a deepened understanding of the fact that actions have consequences. Perhaps more importantly, youngsters learn that it is not possible to live in a family without each person's actions affecting every other person, including themselves. To a degree, each family member reaps what the others sow, and vice versa. Knowing this serves as a powerful motivation for genuine cooperation and mutual caring.

Constructive thinking. Since Family Meetings diminish the amount of energy spent in punishment, "lectures," and squabbling, more and calmer energy can be spent finding solutions to personal and family problems. Constructive thinking takes place because there is an attentive audience (the family) and an agreed-upon procedure (the meeting rules). Also there tends to be much less energy spent in guilt, recriminations, blaming, and hostility. Family Meetings allow you to "get on with it"!

Accountability. Family Meetings help each member to learn to take responsibility for her or his promises and actions. Accountability not only includes agreements (the substance of Family Meetings) but follow-up and completion. Family Meetings make following up issues from a previous meeting a breeze compared to the difficulties experienced by many parents who do not have meetings.

Justice. Family Meetings are not primarily intended to serve as a family courtroom. However, after a family has established the Family Meeting procedure with positivity and buoyancy, Family Meetings can serve beautifully and effectively as both judge and jury for discipline of misconduct or unfairness on the part of any family member. Children learn that as time goes on they are more likely to have real justice from group decisions. Justice as a group function is more likely to be fair, since individual and personal biases are lessened in a family decision. Family Meetings effectively do away with one-to-one retaliation. The degree of fairness and sensitivity acquired by children through Family Meetings is great and cannot be overemphasized.

Teamwork. Family Meetings teach children principles of cooperation and teamwork that might not be learned as effectively otherwise. Parents discover more about themselves as parents and as team members right along with their children. Communication and understanding often increase quite unconsciously as Family Meetings progress. When it appears that one child in particular is having or causing trouble, the amplification of problems that come from being identified as a special "case" are softened and balanced through the teamwork of Family Meetings. Parents are surprised and delighted as from time to time the emerging morality of childhood shines brightly through the unfolding of Family Meetings.

Easier parenting. Although Family Meetings take time and commitment, the effect is a savings of time, energy, stress, and strain to all concerned. The net gain is huge!

QUESTIONS AND ANSWERS

Q. What's the first step in having Family Meetings?

A. Commitment.

Family Meetings take commitment, willingness to press through resistance and maintain continuity. Why waste energy beginning if you're not going to follow through?

Q. What's the second step?

A. Talk it up to the kids!

To the height of your ability, entice, lure, encourage, and charm your children into the discipline and fun of Family Meetings. With equal vigor avoid pressure, intimidation, and coercion about Family Meetings. The children's input should be requested right away. What meeting time, place, and topics are each of the youngsters interested in? Get their interest before imposing any form on anyone.

Q. What's the third step?

A. Planning and agenda.

Give some thought to gauging meetings to meet your family's needs. If your children are spread out over the years, the attention span of the youngest will determine the meeting length. Nevertheless, some topics should be gauged for the oldest so as to keep their interest. Plan your parental agenda for each Family Meeting in advance. Have a concept of what you want to see happen at the meeting without pushing it on anyone. Think of just one or two concrete problems to deal with, like Johnny's getting home on time, Mom's aerobics class, or Sally's prom dress. Keep the focus simple and stick to it. In one of your early meetings discuss your authority as parents. What rights should parents have to apply rules or consequences without taking the matter to a Family Meeting? For instance, perhaps you should have the right to send a child to his room to think a "good thought," entirely at your own discretion. See if you can reason with your children so they will voluntarily accept certain discretionary authority as part of your appropriate parental power. Finally, what sort of activity, that the whole family will enjoy, can you all do right after the meeting? (Ask the kids.)

Q. What if I want Family Meetings but my spouse doesn't?

A. Lovingly overcome resistance.

You might ask, "How could a thinking person not want good family relations? Who would not take the easy way to avoid some of the great trials of childhood and adolescence?" A spouse may block Family Meetings owing to preconceptions, misconceptions, or ignorance. Rather than precipitating a confrontation, take your time. Time is on your side. If you have to wait a week, a month, or a year, but you eventually have Family Meetings, that is what counts. For instance, if it is Mom reading now, look for the points you think will attract your husband. For example, sometimes fathers manage to be workaholics or otherwise avoid most of the tussles with the children. What will he get out of Family Meetings? Take your time and with love and forethought win your spouse's interest.

Q. How old should our children be to have Family Meetings?

A. Four to six years or older.

Four is usually a ripe age to begin Family Meetings. It depends more on the maturity of your youngsters than on their ages. The earlier you start, the better. Once chil-

dren have developed language, embryonic meetings can begin anytime. Develop the ground work for Family Meetings slowly and gradually. It is important for children to acquire a positive association for meetings, even if a meeting doesn't seem productive at the time. Meetings can really come into swing when kids reach five or six and begin to make their own moral choices. Ideally, Family Meetings should be started before your oldest child is seven. But if your children are older and you've had no Family Meetings up to now, or only a few, don't hesitate, start now! It's never too late.

Q. What are the rules of Family Meetings?

A. Consensus and abiding by decisions.

If you will just agree to two simple rules, you will be assured of success.

RULE 1. Consensus—every family decision must have the voluntary consent of every family member.

RULE 2. Decision obligation—everyone agrees to abide by family decisions.

Beyond these two "cardinal" rules, your family is free to have as few or as many rules as you can all agree to.

Q. When should we have our first meeting?

A. This week.

Why not go ahead and have a meeting this week, just to discuss meeting times and topics, and then go see a movie or something you know everyone will enjoy? If you are just beginning Family Meetings, it is best not to hold the first meeting just to solve a family crisis. Don't try to make your Family Meeting a courtroom until after you have established meetings as fun and not punishing. Build the foundations of your meetings on firm positive ground and they will soon serve you in any crisis that may arise.

Q. What should we accomplish at our first meeting?

A. One decision.

Gauge how much your own family can handle, but if you just discuss one topic like allowances, parents' rights, chores, or bedtime, and if you log just one family decision, you have planted a seed that will bear much fruit. It is usually a good idea to discuss ground rules and each person's weekly responsibilities first, with specific rewards and consequences spelled out in advance. Work toward quality rather than quantity in your results. Be sure to agree on a regular meeting time before the end of your first Family Meeting.

Q. What should we know about our second meeting?

A. Work, fairness, and play.

Again, the meeting should just precede some fun event, game, meal, or other activity everyone relishes. First decide who is going to take notes and who is going to conduct the meeting this time. Pull out the family log or journal and review last week's meeting notes. Is there business to be followed up? Were agreements made last week that were to be checked this week to see if they were kept? Are there consequences to be thought up and decided upon? Does anyone have something to discuss or express? The person conducting the meeting should remember to turn to each person and ask for their vote on any decision. In a five member family, the form might work like this: "Nancy, do you agree that we will have no TV Monday night so you can study? Robert, do you agree to give up TV Monday night? Jimmy, do you? Don is that okay with you? It is okay with me." Be sure to get a clear "yes" or "no" answer from each person and state out loud your own vote. Log it.

Q. What should the parents' role be in a Family Meeting?

A. Friends, guides, and peers.

Behind the scenes, you are to nurture, guide, and motivate Family Meetings. Family Meetings won't keep afloat unless one or both parents keep working on them. The trick is to woo and seduce your family through the critical first steps. Soon the usefulness, satisfactions, and value of meetings will have begun to dawn on your family, and your job will ease up. Within Family Meetings, parents are parents, but they serve their children as peers in voting power. ***It is very important in meetings that things applied to the children also be applied to the parents whenever possible.*** For example, parents should also take turns discussing their weekly activities and duties.

Q. What if one family member can't attend regularly?

A. A proxy may work, or return to step one.

Proxy votes work fine for a few missed meetings. Beyond that you should return to step one, commitment. If one or the other parent or an older youngster doesn't take the meetings seriously, the whole process may be undermined. This is why spousal agreement and priority recognition is so important early on. It's not likely that anyone else will give your meetings priority or cause them to happen if you don't. Commitment usually comes when you think through the implications of Family Meetings and gain insight into the very real advantages of them, even to the seemingly least affected family member. Poor attendance can be less trouble if an absent family member agrees not to overturn the family decisions he or she has missed out on. Perhaps you can get agreement from your entire family that an absent person is required to follow Family Meeting decisions for the meetings missed, even though he or she missed the opportunity to vote. This approach is likely to provide some incentive to attend meetings regularly.

Q. What role does punishment play in the meeting process?

A. None.

Doesn't "punishment" connote something painful and demeaning? It often confuses the person with his or her conduct. Why not experiment with using the term "consequence" or some other word that minimizes the negative tone about "punishment"? Since both you and your children will be learning some things by trial and error for a long, long time to come, it doesn't make sense to punish the learning process with "punishment." Children learn that there can be a sense of dignity to accepting "consequences." The usual resistance and defensiveness to correcting a mistake or making amends diminishes. It is heart-warming to watch children learn to accept failure gracefully and then move on without becoming stuck in an emotional snarl.

Q. What are some useful consequences?

A. Natural ones, meaningful ones.

Ideally, consequences should emerge naturally out of the situation. If a youngster puts his hand in a flame there is an immediate and very natural burning consequence. The immediacy of the consequence is just as important as the consequence itself, especially with young children. Often the natural consequences to our children's behavior appear only after such a prolonged period of time that the relevant immediate learning does not take place. One of the greatest challenges of Family Meetings is to provide workable, meaningful, and acceptable consequences. Work or task accomplishment can serve as a valuable consequence only if its meaning is clearly understood by the offending party. Avoid having youngsters dislike a certain job because it has served as punishment. For instance, if Robert is to sweep the garage for a consequence, make sure to clarify the meaning of what he is doing so he doesn't wind up resenting the broom. Make consequences a matter-of-fact learning process without negativity, and you'll be amazed at the quick learning and improved morale that results.

Q. Are parents also subject to consequences?

A. Yes.

Consequences are only a part of a Family Meeting if your family agrees. Parents should be willing to take consensus consequences, and, as role models, should do so cheerfully. Children are very sensitive to double standards, and it is absolutely essential that children can rely on the consistency of the Family Meeting process. For example, Robert's Dad made an agreement to take him to a horse show but Dad reneged at the last moment owing to a business engagement he had forgotten. At the next Family Meeting, the whole family agreed that Dad should sweep the garage for Robert for one week and also take Robert to the next available horse show. Even a hint that Family Meeting rules work only at the whim of the parents, who can pull rank at any moment, seriously corrupts the process and wreaks havoc with weeks of hard work.

Q. What should be kept in the family notebook?

A. Date
Note-taker
Roll
Decisions

The essentials seem to be the date, the name of the note-keeper for that meeting, who is present, and the decisions the family has agreed upon. You may wish to take notes on what each person says, anything you discuss, or whatever needs a follow-up. Sometimes you will want each family member to sign the notebook next to an agreement they have made. Be creative, draw pictures, doodle, tailor your journal to your family. Don't underestimate the importance of keeping notes. Your log will prove itself to you in time and give you a valuable perspective on your family that you could obtain in no other way.

Q. How often should we hold Family Meetings?

A. Weekly.

Most families find weekly meetings work best. With younger children, spanning more than a week between meetings makes the last meeting seem like ancient history. Meaningful follow-up becomes more difficult. Ultimately, it is up to your family to decide what fits your particular needs. It is better to decide on a regular schedule in advance, rather than going from meeting to meeting. Regular habits make the process easier. Prearrange with your family (by agreement, of course) to have some discretion so that you can call an emergency meeting occasionally. (Remember to log all your meetings.) Some family crises just won't wait a week. There is nothing to keep you from having a Family Meeting daily if need be.

Q. What are some pitfalls of Family Meetings?

A. Monotony and resistance.

Having to do with the nitty-gritty of family life, Family Meetings can seem all too unglamorous. Keep in mind, the benefits of Family Meetings are mostly long term, not short term. Sometimes Family Meetings become routine, monotonous, and boring. Things may seem to be running too smoothly; there's nothing to bring up at a meeting. Great resistance sets in, and although there may be lip service to their value, meetings just never seem to happen. This is where your creativity and ingenuity come in. However much resistance you have to plow through, do it. Later on, you may be able to have very brief but effective meetings, once everyone has caught on and learned ways to get something from the process.

Q. Will we always need to have meetings every week?

A. No.

A relieving and refreshing side benefit is that meetings get easier and easier as you proceed. After precedents and habits have been established, you can skip up to several weeks and still have everything running smoothly. This is why it is so important to do things well at the outset. Have regular, consistent, and fun meetings at first and you will experience the payoff for years. Once you get the family ship under way, it will continue almost of its own momentum. Be sure that the rudder is headed in the right direction at the launching, and navigation will be easier from then on!

Q. What do we do if after a few meetings, the kids turn off to them?

A. Don't give up.

Look for the obvious. Are meetings too punishing or long for the children? Is fairness alive and well at your meetings? The children may want to get the meeting over with so they can go swimming. Fine. Shorten the meeting, but make sure it comes before swimming. Kids get very fast and efficient when a powerful reward follows their efforts. It may help to change the name or format of the meetings. Since there are only two cardinal rules of Family Meetings, consensus and decision obligation, this gives you more flexibility than you are probably aware of. For example, casually talk about an issue at the supper table, night by night. When you have agreement, log it. If necessary, approach each person, one-to-one, to get agreement. Log it. Family Meetings can succeed despite the most monumental odds. Remember, Family Meetings are ten percent instigation and ninety percent inspiration.

Q. What if one youngster regularly disrupts meetings?

A. Press on.

Discuss it; air feelings; listen carefully to everyone; find relevant consequences; get agreement; follow-up next week. Look for what payoffs the child derives from "acting out." Is it a call for attention? Is it anger? Maybe a meeting could be devoted just to being silly. Through talk and compromise the child may be able to keep a simple agreement about his or her meeting behavior. Be sure to praise strongly or reward tangibly any time or effort spent in good behavior. Most of all, don't give up. The greatest patience is required in these early meetings, but as time passes, the payoffs mount up.

Q. Do we have to plan a special, fun event for every meeting?

A. Yes and no.

Regular, positive rewards are most important during the early phases of Family Meetings, then you can go to intermittent rewards. Remember the principle: rewarded attitudes and actions will flourish; unrewarded conduct will pass away.

Q. What educational goals especially apply to Family Meetings?

A. Sexuality and spirituality.

A tremendous amount of learning will take place quite unconsciously. Kids learn to pay attention, listen, bargain, communicate, be comfortable with an audience, take notes, be more accountable, have consideration, understand each other: the list is endless. There are two subjects that I have found from experience to be uniquely appropriate to Family Meetings. These are human sexuality and religion. As in all matters, your family has complete control over what is included in Family Meetings under either of these topics.

Q. Is it worthwhile to start Family Meetings during the teens?

A. Yes.

It is usually easier if children learn about consensus and abiding decisions early in life, but please note, IT IS NEVER TOO LATE! It is much easier to initiate meetings during a lull in family crises. Get the positive tone going. Be patient, even teenagers won't learn the process overnight, nor will they immediately trust it. In the teens you can take up such important matters as how long it is appropriate for children to live at home.

Q. Are there other forms of Family Meetings?

A. Yes.

In informal ways, families may be having Family Meetings without even realizing it. Over many years, numerous churches and other organizations have sponsored various forms of Family Meetings, "family night," "home night," or "firesides." This particular structure with its two cardinal rules is offered to you simply because it has withstood the test of time and direct experience. Feel free to be innovative with the structure of Family Meetings so they really suit your particular family.

Q. What about single parents and alternative families?

A. Up threefold in ten years.

Non-traditional families are so prevalent now that the need for a solid and workable Family Meeting structure with interfamily networking is greater than ever. Family Meetings are a powerful stabilizing force that often makes the difference between a family being in or out of control. Single parents, foster children, extended families, and other family situations are discussed in the next section, "Family Meetings with Different Types of Families."

Q. What should I do in case of . . . ?

A. Ask at your next Family Meeting.

Almost every question that arises with your children can literally be taken to your next Family Meeting. When something comes up that you feel perplexed about, first talk to your spouse and then take it back to the next meeting and ask for your family's counsel. For example, the Applebee family agreed that if someone said or did something that seemed to cause hurt feelings, the "injured party" would go immediately and silently to his room, close the door, and take "alone time." Several days after this agreement, twelve-year-old Doreen got in a tiff with her mom about wearing her mom's jewelry. Mom was mad because Doreen had worn her antique pearls without asking. Mom had then refused jewelry to Doreen, and had tried to end the dispute by saying, ". . . because I say so!" Doreen called her mom "a hurtful name." Doreen got slapped, then tearfully complained that her mom had broken the Family Meeting agreement to go to her room. Mom had very mixed feelings, and asked, "What should I do in this case?" The answer ever and again is to have a meeting and bring up the issue. Before you take your case to the Family Meeting, ask yourself, "What do I really want here: power, a consequence, or something else?"

FAMILY MEETINGS WITH DIFFERENT TYPES OF FAMILIES

The Single Child Family

Parents of an only child sometimes feel that Family Meetings are unnecessary. Things may run smoothly. The child behaves well. Little discipline is needed, and when it is applied, the child readily responds. Why bother with Family Meetings? One reason is that Family Meetings are valuable insurance for the future. Moreover, a one child family may be heavily weighted toward the preferences of the parents, no matter how loving and fair the parents intend to be. Or, it may be overly weighted toward the wishes of the child, who does not have to share parental attention with other siblings. Sometimes an only child does not feel the sense of family and kindredness that she would feel among brothers and sisters. Here is where Family Meetings come in. The child develops a sense of family identity through meetings. In Family Meetings with just one youngster, both parents should enact the role of peer in voting power with great care. The youngster's will and decision power should be nurtured. The emotions of two adults can easily overpower a child so that it is difficult to know how much freedom of will the youngster is experiencing. Kids like to please. But, votes in Family Meetings should do more than merely please the parents. A child's vote should honestly reflect the views and wishes of the child.

Two Young Children

You can start enacting the *form* of Family Meetings when the children are still quite young. Even when the older child is only three or four, a brief meeting can be held each week with the smaller youngster in the arms of a parent. A valuable technique at such embryonic meetings is to ask both children (at least the one that is beginning to talk) to say or do just one thing. For instance, "If you had two wishes in the whole wide world, what would they be?" If there is an answer, put it in the family notebook. Next, explain that everyone is going to sit quietly for just a moment and think one "good thought." "What makes you happy?" "What did you play that was fun yesterday?" Then, have everyone hold hands and close their eyes briefly for the experience of quiet time. Afterwards, share "good thoughts," with Mom and Dad also participating. Help the little ones think back on some good moments by reminding them of things they did that were fun. In this way children learn, meeting by meeting, to think good thoughts easily and naturally. Establish a routine of taking a few minutes just to sit together, and before long you will be having a Family Meeting.

With very young children it is important that the parents be in charge of Family Meetings. The kids may have to be directed, managed, and told what to do. Such directing and managing should give way to consensual agreements as soon as your children develop language and reasoning skills. Most children can understand the meaning of consensus by three to five years of age, and they should be given full charge of their voting power by that time. Parents should select topics for the meetings that they agree are appropriate for the kids and that will assist them to learn the Family Meeting process. The transition from benevolent autocracy to consensual Family Council should be gradual. Pick topics and issues so the child can make mistakes and can learn from those mistakes joyfully and without too much disappointment. Note: once you have begun to hand over voting power to a youngster, never take it back without the agreement and understanding of the child concerned. If a child fears that you will arbitrarily upturn his voting power, he loses trust that the "power" is really his at all.

Two Older Children or Teenagers

The ease and success of your Family Meetings will depend in part on your family dynamics. What habits have already been formed by you and your older children up to this point? What alliances have already been formed within your family? Who runs the family? Who gets his or her way? Who doesn't? If you have a reasonably comfortable relationship with your teenagers, Family Meetings may flow quite naturally. Teenagers may be harder to convince. Why is it worth their time? What's in it for them? Some teenagers seem to be gone all of the time. They are often outwardly directed and feel they are moving out of family activities, not into them. Family Meetings may be just what you need to keep abreast of later childhood and the teens. Since teenagers are often heavily influenced by peers and the media, Family Meetings will draw them back into a sense of family identity and family unity.

Consider ways to make the Family Meeting process relevant to your older youngsters. Rights and privileges are usually so important to teenagers that Family Meetings will appeal to them, if you take pains in describing and explaining the process. What teenager doesn't want more freedom? And what better place than Family Meetings lovingly to pace expanding liberties? Teenagers need to be acknowledged and respected for the levels of maturity they have attained, regardless of how parents perceive their maturity. So much change, strong hormones, and confusion attend the teen years that the supportive but non-coercive environment of Family Meetings can serve as a superlative forum for ironing out nearly every problem and difficulty.

With Family Meetings during adolescence, the core factor is trust. You can assist your youngster to trust the meeting process by being even more vigilant to consistency and fairness. Sometimes it is helpful to develop a confidentiality agreement that applies to Family Meet-

ings. If you have allowed for and kept "family secrets" over the years, your teenager may more readily open up during Family Meetings to reveal some of those personal issues that are experienced so poignantly during adolescence. Family Meetings can greatly reduce the intensity of conflicts over power and authority, since in meetings everyone functions as equals. Authority is not taken and held over a teenager. It comes from the family as a whole and is authored, in part, by the very teenager who might otherwise be in grave conflict with authority.

One Young Child and One Much Older

From the point of view of youngsters who may be many years junior or senior to their brothers and sisters, it can seem as though they have had quite different upbringings, even different parents. Family Meetings help to unify disparate families without imposing uniformity on anyone. One of the delightful scenes of family life is to glimpse the older children skillfully and caringly passing on something they have learned to those just a little younger, and those younger ones eagerly receiving and passing their new found treasures on to still younger ones.

If you have difficulty getting your older child to come to meetings, appeal to her as a peer, explain that her contribution is really needed to allow the meetings to work. Perhaps you can get consensus to form a subcommittee. The younger child and both parents would work out most matters that don't concern the older child. This may relieve some of the boredom the older youngster might experience if every detail of business with the younger child had to be handled in Family Meetings. Let Family Meetings truly maximize the enjoyment of everyone being together.

Three Children in a Family

In most cases, the three child family is ideally suited for Family Meetings. Consensus can work very efficiently with five people. In a five member family, one child is always the eldest, one in the middle, and one the youngest. Certain inevitabilities follow. For example, for about a year or so the first born child has no brothers or sisters. The parents may have no experience in childrearing. The middle child may be just that—in the middle. A middle child may feel less distinction than the other two. The youngest child is often the "baby" who always had older siblings and special attention (or neglect). Family Meetings are uniquely suited to level out some of the effects of being one of three brothers and sisters. If the oldest youngster tends to be too serious, Family Meetings can be used to reward those activities that lead to more relaxation and flexibility. If the middle child is a day-dreamer, Family Meetings will add order and structure to his life. If the youngest one is happy-go-lucky but tends to be irresponsible, then Family Meetings can assist that child to continue to be happy while becoming more personally accountable, meeting by meeting.

Larger Families

The value of Family Meetings becomes even greater with larger families. With more children, Family Meetings insure a better chance for everyone to get a fair shake. The more family members, the less of Mom's and Dad's attention goes to any particular child, all else being equal. Family Meetings provide a structure to organize the family and employ the services of older children on behalf of their younger sisters and brothers. The larger your family is, the more good attendance and good family notes will help your Family Meetings. Family Meetings allow the division of labor, essential in a sizable family, to be assigned fairly and equitably. As you add family members, consensus becomes more cumbersome, so that for more than about twelve members a more sophisticated model of family governance should be applied. If you have a very large family, use your consensual process to invoke a more efficient model of governance. By consensus you can relegate some decisions to a "majority rule" model, or by consensus develop subcommittees with power of their own. In this way you can avoid having every "stitch" of family life threaded through time-consuming consensual discussions. Be inventive. Whatever type of family government you choose, choose it by consensus.

Families by Marriage or Life-style

Family Meetings have great stabilizing and cohesive power in those circumstances where children are not genetically related for one reason or another. Consider the following example. Helen and Bob were a couple in their late thirties with three children between them. Helen had been married previously, and after many years of unsuccessful attempts at conception, she and her former husband decided to adopt a seven-year-old Vietnamese orphan named Lee. Although they had been well-intentioned in their adoption plans, the youngster was a great trial to this inexperienced couple. Troubles snowballed, and within two years they had divorced. Helen won custody of Lee, whom she genuinely loved but had difficulty controlling. Bob had two children from his former marriage, Janet (age six), and Tony (age five). Helen wanted very much to have Family Meetings to solve numerous difficulties she was experiencing with her new family. Although the kids knew each other for about seven months while Bob and Helen were dating, they had only lived together under one roof for about five weeks. Life was hectic. Lee was most resistant to Family Meetings. He was afraid everyone would gang up on him. It wasn't that the kids fought so much as that Janet and Tony were afraid of Lee.

Meanwhile, Lee ignored Janet and Tony all that he could. Secretly, Bob didn't like Lee very well and felt that he was undisciplined and out of Helen's control much of the time. Helen acquired a sense of what the resistances were to meetings. First, she worked on Bob and pointed out that the family situation couldn't go on unchanged without escalating their grief. After some more persuasive explanation on Helen's part, Bob made a commitment to try Family Meetings for ten sessions. He also agreed to try and handle their hassles with the children outside the Family Meetings at least for the first few weeks. Knowing that Lee wanted a pet dog gave Bob and Helen some bargaining power to gain Lee's attendance and cooperation. Janet and Tony went along with meetings but were very slow at keeping their agreements to share family chores. Time and effort paid off, and after seven meetings all the kids said they liked Family Meetings. The younger kids were doing more to take care of their toys and clothes, and Lee was minding his mom better. The family reached consensus that after that week's meeting everyone would go to pick out a puppy that Lee had agreed to feed and train. Although Bob still didn't like Lee very well, he had grown more tolerant of this boy and they had struck up some good conversations after Family Meetings about kinds of dogs and which ones make the best watchdogs.

Family Meetings are extremely powerful in families by marriage or life-style because the meetings give everyone a common ground from which to relate. Prejudice and feelings about race, sex, age, and past training are diminished because the power of your vote in a family meeting has nothing to do with these traits. Attention to and treatment of the kids is more fairly and equally applied to each youngster.

Live-in Relatives and Other Folks

Family Meetings are designed to include everyone that lives together under one roof. If Grandmother or Aunt Edith live with you, by all means include them in Family Meetings. Relatives or other folks that live with you for more than a vacation should participate in the Family Meetings just like any other family member. Decisions and consensus should apply to them just like to Mom and Dad and the kids. If you want someone who does not live with you to attend Family Meetings, fine. Be aware that in a sense the family *has* to live together, *has* to share mutual "reaping" of what any family member has "sown." These are the forces that allow Family Meetings to work in practice as well as in theory. Outsiders may be much less affected by these forces and thereby less prone to take your meetings seriously.

Families with Shared Child Custody

If you are in a situation where you take your children a few days or a few weeks at a time, Family Meetings can work for you, too. Are your children between homes? Perhaps the kids seem neither with you nor with your ex-partner long enough for useful Family Meetings. As you know, the children are likely to be off-balance or in shock if there has been a recent separation or divorce. Some time must pass for children to catch up with the adjustments forced upon them by their new lives. Family Meetings can greatly lessen the tragedy and hardship of divorce. If you had Family Meetings prior to your separation they can serve as a living bridge of continuity. The children can cross more safely over the turbulent waters of your marital dissolution. There may be heartache that Mom or Dad is gone, but Family Meeting decisions and the consensual process remain unchanged. What a valuable refuge for children at a time when their lives seem turned upside down.

Much of the previous portrayal of Family Meetings applies to families in transition. The best arrangement is to get agreement with the estranged parent so that the rules and expectations of one household are compatible with those of the other household. Family Meetings with both households once a month or so will alleviate double standards and miscommunications. If there are new partners, they should be included if they are willing. The bitterness and sorrow of divorce, or possessiveness and jealousy with new partners may stand in the way of blended-Family Meetings. Don't be too discouraged; time is still on your side. Press on with Family Meetings as a single parent if need be.

If you've not had Family Meetings before, start now. Your "ex" may seem to sabotage your efforts for a while. Don't worry, usually this will pass, especially if you sincerely convey the value of Family Meetings to your "ex." He or she will be more likely to cooperate with your Family Meeting endeavors if the benefits to both children and parents are clearly communicated. When you have visitation privileges, first give the kids time to readjust to being with you again, then hold a Family Meeting. Have your Family Meeting decisions apply primarily to the time (days or weeks) your children are living with you. Have a second Family Meeting just before your ex-spouse takes them again. It will work best if the children are under the jurisdiction of just one set of family rules. But, if your "ex" wants separate meetings, or none at all, go ahead and have them on your own. If you keep the two cardinal rules, it will still be well worth your efforts. Family Meetings are remarkably adaptable.

Weekend Visitation

If you are a father or mother, recently divorced, with visitation rights to see your children only two weekends per month and three weeks in the summer, Family Meetings can be a reassuring and calming salve. It's a painful and humbling realization that you can't see your children more often than the court allows. Not seeing them hurts, yet seeing them sometimes is very painful, too. Visitation after days or weeks of absence sometimes brings back a flood of painful memories. It's a small wonder that some mothers and fathers neglect their visiting privileges. ***Many things can't survive divorce; Family Meetings can.*** Mom or Dad may not be present now, but Family Meetings can go on.

Two Family Meetings per weekend are recommended for parents who want the most from their visiting times and who sincerely want the best for their offspring. Have a meeting soon after you pick up your kids. Discuss the weekend. What do the children want and expect from their time with Dad or Mom? Work by consensus. Be patient, don't pull rank! Have a second brief meeting before they go back to the other parent. Think back over the weekend with the kids. Talk in the meeting about one event that each person enjoyed. What was one funny thing that took place this visit? By beginning and ending your visitation periods with these brief meetings, you establish a beneficial ritual to maximize the success of your childrens' adjustment to their new lives with Mom and Dad living apart. Don't forget to keep notes.

Single Parents

Although some single parents fare quite well with their circumstances, imagine the plight of others. You have three small children. Suddenly you find yourself bereft of your partner. You have few job skills. You have to keep up with all of the household tasks. You have new burdens you hadn't dreamed of. You have no money. You have payments to be made. You feel lost, lonely, panicky, and worthless. The sheer circumstances of life are nearly crushing. This real-life tragedy is repeated millions upon millions of times in our culture. What can be done? For some couples, the time for an ounce of prevention is gone. But, the prospect of a future of Family Meetings is still there. Take that prospect and turn it into a reality. Family Meetings are one of the ways to regain a strong sense of family unity with just you and your children. Children progress best with two cooperative parents. Family Meetings allow you to compensate for some of what is missing if your partner has left you. Take advantage of Family Meetings. The ease of becoming ungrounded and losing your common sense perspective is a very real danger in single parenting. Even if you chose to be a single parent by adopting or arranging your pregnancy, have Family Meetings; they will stand you in good stead. The extremes of mutual dependency between you and your children, the moments of being at wits' end, the missing discipline, the difficulties your children have with your new lover, or your own lonely nights can be sensibly balanced out through Family Meetings.

As a single parent, be sure to give your meetings some structure to distinguish them from other home activities. Give your Family Meetings a name, whatever you and your children like, and then refer to them by name. Be slightly formal in keeping notes to emphasize the importance of your Family Meeting notebook. Share note-taking with your children if they are old enough to write clearly. The greatest challenge is to be consistent and stick to the rules without deviation.

It will be wise to do some serious thinking about your relation with your children. Who runs whom? Who trains whom? What do you fear about your children? Are you vulnerable to manipulation by one or more of your kids because of something you fear about them? Think

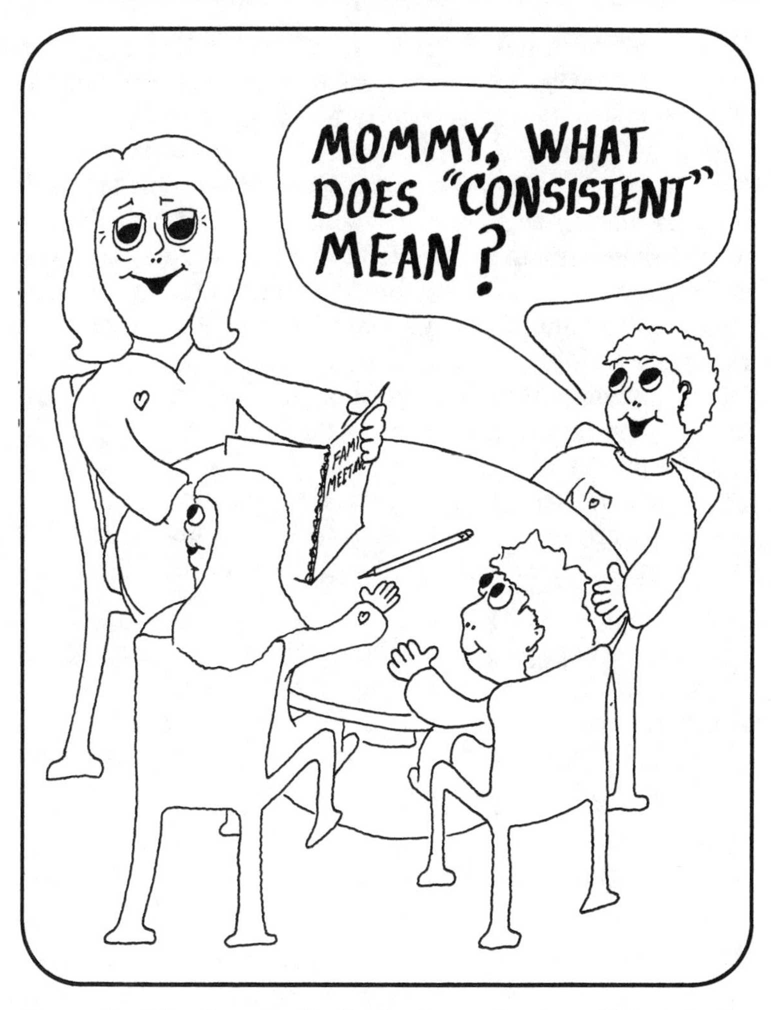

through this fear to its logical conclusion. What is the worst case? Face it. Is there something you need that your children provide? Are you afraid of losing their affection? Consider what you can do to get your needs met with your children in the most constructive way possible.

Now consider what power or leverage you have with your children. Be practical. What do your children need or want that only you can provide? Make a list. What do they want that they could get elsewhere but are likely to come to you for? What powerful reward can you give or withhold as an incentive for participating in Family

Meetings? As tough as it is, this type of thinking may be your salvation in the months to come. Use everything in your power to cause Family Meetings to be a success. If you feel you are losing control of your children and Family Meetings seem to have little effect, don't stop. It may be necessary to ask a friend, neighbor, relative, or older adolescent to sit in on your Family Meetings as a stabilizing and balancing force to complement your presence. Think about it. Who do you know that has the maturity and love of children to assist you in this way? How can you compensate this person for his or her services? Be sure you get a commitment of weeks or months that he or she will participate in your Family Meetings. Be sure the person understands the procedure. Don't forget to obtain your children's agreement about inviting this person. Take this step, it can make all the difference in the world.

Remember, you are bigger, stronger, older, more knowledgeable, and more experienced than any of your children. Despite pressing hardships, you do have the power and strength to convince your children to have meetings and make them work. Do it.

MEMORABLE ANECDOTES

Some of the stories that follow are composites gleaned from many different families I have seen as a family therapist. Some of these gleanings are nearly direct quotations from various participants in Family Meetings. In these cases, intimate family episodes are revealed here by permission of the families involved. Some of the names and facts have been changed to respect the privacy of individuals concerned. All of these anecdotes are based on the real life experiences of families who have experimented with the Family Meeting process.

New Beginnings

Paula had great and idealistic expectations of marriage. Yet within a year after her marriage to George, their relationship was fraught with trouble. George started coming home from work later and later as the weeks wore on. Whenever Paula complained, George would get angry and tell her he didn't want to talk about it. Or, he'd dismiss the subject by saying, "I was just at the bar having a beer with the guys from work." Paula felt lonely a lot during her pregnancy, and it seemed only natural that she would turn to her newborn daughter for companionship and affection. When George suddenly left Paula, the next year, Paula was devastated. She clung all the more desperately to her young daughter. Paula's life seemed to take another downhill turn when she was abruptly laid off from her teaching job. The child care center where she left Cathy four hours per day had no more funding and her babysitting expenses went out of sight. Reluctantly, Paula went on county support. At this point Paula felt more insecure than ever. Her neediness prompted her to do almost anything in her power to please her three-year-old daughter. At times it seemed that Cathy was the only person in the world who loved Paula, and vice versa. Without realizing it, Paula gave way to nearly every one of Cathy's whims. Visitors noticed the inordinate amount of time it took Paula to get Cathy to do anything. Cathy would drag out dressing or brushing her teeth for so long that a visitor would nearly scream. Friends tried to tell Paula that things had gotten out of hand with her daughter, but she would become all the more defensive of her relationship to Cathy.

After a few more months, Cathy began refusing to go to nursery school or to stay with babysitters. Paula's health broke when a lingering cough progressed into pneumonia. While in the hospital, Paula had the realization that she absolutely had to find a way to change the situation with Cathy. After talking earnestly to a friend at the hospital, she vowed that she would start Family Meetings with Cathy as soon as she got home.

Paula read some materials on Family Meetings and talked to Cathy about the two of them having "meetings" to talk about the week and plan their activities. Cathy, who was now four, was agreeable at the first Family Meeting. Their agreements included Cathy doing things more quickly, not whining, and obeying Paula. As promised, Paula took Cathy to the zoo after their meeting. For a few hours, Cathy actually kept her Family Meeting agreements, but as the week wore on, Cathy slipped more and more into the old pattern. She became more demanding. Paula began giving in to avoid the unpleasantness with her child. Later in the week, Paula attempted another meeting with Cathy. It proved very difficult to keep a matter-of-fact and businesslike tone with Cathy. Cathy would become silly whenever Paula asked about last week's agreements. She continued to be so silly that the meeting was aborted. Paula felt so behind since her time at the hospital that several weeks slipped by with no further efforts at Family Meetings. Paula felt guilty. This served only to make her feel more defeated about taking up meetings again. After a few more weeks Cathy was refusing to do almost anything she was asked. Paula was at her wits' end more than ever. Her friend suggested that she find an outside person to sit in on Family Meetings. Who would it be? There didn't seem to be anyone she felt comfortable asking. Cathy would agree to someone, then change her mind after a few minutes.

Paula knew a neighbor, Ann, who also was a single parent with two older children. Until now they hadn't seemed to have much in common since their children differed so much in age. Paula took up her courage and approached her neighbor about Family Meetings. The talk relieved Paula. They agreed to sit in on each other's Family Meetings, keeping open the possibility of trying a meeting with all the children together. Ann insisted that Paula have a babysitter for Cathy when she attended Ann's Family Meetings. Having taken this step, Paula felt better and even became a little firmer with Cathy.

The first meeting with Ann, Paula, and Cathy was another silly one where Cathy seemed only interested in showing off for a new person. They aborted the meeting with little accomplished. However, when it came time to go swimming after the meeting, both Ann and Paula reminded Cathy that going swimming depended on Cathy's cooperation at the meeting. Cathy started screaming, but they did not go swimming. This was a big accomplishment for Paula, who would ordinarily have allowed Cathy to manipulate her into taking her swimming anyway. Later, the two women agreed to give Family Meetings another try while sticking to the cardinal meeting rules.

Cathy was more resistant than ever to the next meeting. She didn't even want Ann in the house. Two more meetings were aborted with whining, crying, and silliness. On the fourth attempt at a meeting, Paula made a special effort to have Cathy rested and in a positive mood just before Ann arrived. During this session, Cathy began to listen and agreed to a few chores around the house. She agreed to brush her teeth and be in bed by 8:30 each night. She agreed to go to nursery school without fussing. Paula agreed to read to her from her favorite book each night. Ann agreed to meet with them again in just three days to check up on these agreements.

Paula had several short talks with Cathy during the next two days. Each time, she would go over with Cathy those things that Cathy was to remember to do that day. She encouraged Cathy without accusing her of wrongdoing and reminded her of how much fun they would have reading that evening. Having two meetings per week for a while helped a lot and kept Cathy more focused on her agreements. The next two weeks went more smoothly. There were a couple of nights when Paula had to withhold reading at bedtime. Cathy cried and carried on, but Paula kept her resolve, partly because she also felt responsibility to Ann, who was in on this agreement and consequence. Paula now began to see how her permissiveness with Cathy had not secured her more love from this youngster at all. She also acquired important experience from sitting in on the Family Meetings with Ann and her boys. Paula was not so dependent on the approval of Ann's boys as she was locked into her own daughter's approval. Now she could see more clearly how children need definite limits and boundaries in their young lives.

The next months were a refreshing improvement for Paula and Cathy, so much so that when Ann and her boys moved away eleven months later, Paula and Cathy were able to conduct their own Family Meetings. Cathy had shifted her mental activities into figuring out how to get what she wanted from Family Meetings, rather than emotionally manipulating her mother. And this had happened more or less naturally and unconsciously.

Secret Fire

"Wesley must have been about five, and our older boy, Scott, about seven. I was working full time and their mom, Betty, was teaching in the mornings. Lately our time with the kids had been a little thin. Betty was upset this particular afternoon and called me aside as soon as I walked in the door from work. She had smelled match smoke in the boys' room earlier that afternoon and after some investigation determined that Wesley had indeed been playing with matches. The boys had been instructed over the years not to play with matches, and we'd really had no trouble up to this time. Apparently Wesley had been secretly doing this for several weeks. Betty and I felt rather undermined, as though we didn't know our little boy as well as we thought we did.

"We'd been having Family Meetings on and off for a few months; we all understood the idea of decisions by consensus. At first, the boys didn't want to come to meetings, but more recently they seemed to like them more, sometimes reminding us to have a Family Meeting. Betty and I had been pretty good about not taking up arbitrary authority over the boys. We were both tempted by the match incident, but agreed that this was something we should handle in a Family Meeting.

"We felt that fire is such a serious danger that an emergency meeting should be called. We asked the boys to come into the kitchen. Scott grumbled a little but came in. Wes was silent and resistant. We were patient but firm about his coming to the meeting. His reluctance made it clear that he sensed that we were on to the secret matches. Finally Wes dragged himself into the meeting in a most distracted state of mind. We read our notes and took care of some preliminary business to set a matter-of-fact, businesslike tone, despite our anxiety about Wesley's playing with fire. Then, by previous arrangement with Betty, I turned to the boys and said, 'How would you like to play with fire?' The boys' eyes got big and they didn't say anything for a minute. Wes appeared somewhat sheepish. He was caught most off guard but before long both boys were chanting that they wanted to play with fire. We then asked, 'Do you fellas think there should be any safety rules about playing with fire?' They cautiously agreed. We posed the question another way, hoping to solicit their more mature natures. 'If you guys were with a much younger child, say three-year-old Sally, would it be safe for her to play with matches?' Now that the spotlight seemed off Wes and on a hypothetical situation, he readily stated that the three-year-old might get burned.

"Next, we asked, 'What safety rules should we have in our family?' After another twenty minutes of discussion the boys had become quite involved in planning to play with fire. We had all agreed on some safety rules: 1) either Betty or I had to be present any time the boys played with fire, 2) the boys were responsible for the 'Fire Department.' Wesley got a big pitcher of water and made a 'Fire Dept' label which he taped on it. Scott got out the metal wok from the kitchen, since it formed a large and fireproof bowl. Betty found a candle, set it in the middle of the wok, and we put the whole business down on the fireproof tile floor. The boys took much delight in gathering up little bits and pieces of cotton fabric, wood, metal, and paper to burn or experiment with. We tried to exclude items that might cause toxic fumes when burned. The boys sat down on either side of the wok with all their paraphernalia, truly excited that they were going to be allowed to play with fire. They had agreed to the safety rules, all flames were to be kept inside the perimeter of the wok, the 'Fire Dept.' was nearby—time to light up.

"Each boy was given a single book of matches. Betty and I sat back to watch over the show. Scott lit the candle, and both he and Wes became totally engrossed in trying to light or burn every imaginable little scrap they had brought in. We had talked at length by this time about smoke, burns, first aid, and many other features of fire safety. Although the boys burned themselves mildly several times, we said nothing. It was quite intriguing to watch them explore this taboo activity. They really learned quite a lot: what would and wouldn't burn, what stayed hot, how a flame could start a fire without touching anything, and how quickly fingers felt heat, too. They were willing to stop after every match in their two books were gone. The boys also made a solemn vow not to play with fire in any way without our presence. We agreed, in turn, that anytime the boys wanted to play with fire they could come and ask, and one of us would (in a timely manner) provide the wok, pitcher, candle,

and the supervision to burn up a book of matches. Betty and I shrank from the thought that we would now be set upon by the boys for a burning party every time we turned around.

"It turned out not to be that way. The boys did ask to play with matches a few more times, but somehow taking away the taboo quality of playing with fire reduced the boys' preoccupation with fire. We used 'playing with fire' as a reward for other good conduct in the future, so it served a double purpose. At our next meeting we were able to get Wes to see how much better it is to ask first. We pointed out how through Family Meetings he usually could get something he wanted, even to play with fire. Looking back, I would say that this incident strengthened our Family Meeting process. Most of all, it short-circuited a lot of potential trouble about playing with fire behind our backs. What they learned from playing with fire seemed to make them more safety conscious. Amazingly, playing with fire never became a big issue in the boys' lives. I cannot remember another incident of either disobedience or carelessness with matches. Later on the boys learned to be good builders of home fires, and they dearly loved to watch the dancing flames."

Father's Law

This is the story of a family that did not attempt to begin Family Meetings until a family crisis had begun to develop.

Sally had just turned fifteen, or perhaps I should say fifteen going on twenty-five. Sally was bright and in many ways sophisticated for her age. As you might expect, there was another part of her that was very much a child. She was very socially inclined and tended to neglect her school work and routine duties. She was attractive and slightly precocious in her physical development. She was eleven and in her father's custody at the time he married her stepmother, Emily, who had two girls of her own, Lisa (age five), and Karie (age eight). Sally got along fairly well with her dad until he married Emily, then things just seemed to fall apart. Emily had a genuine affection for Sally and they got on rather well. Sally had seemed defensive of her personal independence from the very outset, so Emily had been very timid in presuming to discipline Jim's daughter. Although Sally seemed to enjoy babysitting her stepsisters, Lisa and Karie, she much preferred to be on her own or with her own friends.

Trouble began between Sally and her dad over her being out too late, who her friends were, her poor performance at school, and what her dad called her "slovenliness" around the house. Things went along alright for a while, with Jim and Sally more or less avoiding each other. They would rarely talk except for a few words at the supper table. This was usually the only time they saw each other during week days. On weekends Jim was often out on call, as his job was one that required him to respond to a radio call beeper on his belt. Emily wanted the family to have Family Meetings. Her hands were full with her two daughters, and she saw the communications between Sally and her husband breaking down daily. The two little girls agreed, but both Jim and Sally were most resistant. Sally said she didn't think it was her stepsisters' business what she did or who her friends were. Besides, they were too young to understand her predicaments as a teenager. Jim stoicly read the example of a Family Meeting, the one with Don, Julie, Nancy, Robert and Jimmy (p.7). He snorted at the end that he didn't think it would work, but said he'd give it a try anyway. He said he wanted things to be better between his daughter, Sally, and him. Emily did some pleading with Sally and promised to help with the matter of her little stepsisters and the differences in their ages and experience.

The first meeting was like pulling teeth. Jim was mostly quiet and Sally hardly said a word. They worked out some agreements about the activities of the little girls, and Sally even agreed to do the dishes she had been neglecting. By the next meeting, Sally still hadn't done her share of the dishes. Eventually, Emily cleaned them up late in the evening. Before the end of the second meeting Jim's beeper sounded and he had to leave early. No meeting took place the next week. Sally half-heartedly did the dishes and was a trial to everyone, according to her stepmother.

In two weeks, one of Sally's friends was having a big shindig for all her teenage pals. There had already been friction between Sally and her dad about boys. She was not permitted to date yet. Nevertheless, Sally had managed to have a few quasi-dates that her dad didn't know about. She represented them to him as "visiting a girlfriend for the evening." First, Sally told her stepmother about the party, saying she was going. When Emily told Jim, he blew up. Jim encountered Sally at dinner and made it clear that Sally was not old enough to go out with boys or to the party. And that was that. Sally stormed out of the dining room in a huff. Silence and distance prevailed the next week. Sally went to the party anyway, against her father's orders. When she got home very late, Jim was boiling. Despite Emily's every effort, Jim became violent with Sally. It was an ugly scene, and although Sally was not physically injured, she felt only bitter resentment for her father when he told her that as long as she was living under his roof and eating his food, she had better do what he said. Otherwise, she could get out.

Sally had run away from home and was living with a nearby relative, a brother-in-law, when I had opportunity to talk with Jim about Family Meetings.

BOB. I understand that this is quite painful for you, Jim. Tell me about Family Meetings, did you give them a go?

JIM. We tried them for a while . . . but, I don't know,

they didn't work. Sally's such a headstrong kid, I can't do anything with her.

BOB. What agreements did you and Sally make in your meetings?

JIM. She promised to do the dishes, like always she left her work for others to do . . . she always thinks she's getting away with something, like right now with my brother-in-law.

BOB. What did you agree to in the Family Meeting, apart from Sally's broken agreement about doing the dishes?

JIM. What do you mean? I thought Family Meetings were to get the kids in line.

BOB. That's part of it, but in Family Meetings the idea is that everyone participates, including the parents. We make agreements by common consensus where everybody agrees or else no decision is made. Did Sally voluntarily agree to do the dishes? And did you all remember to agree on a reward or consequence for doing or not doing the dishes?

JIM (*getting irritated*). Well, I don't go along with that. Kids should do what their parents tell them to, regardless. What are we coming to, that we should bribe and sweet-talk our own kids into doing a few chores we tell them to do?

BOB. When you and Emily first started Family Meetings, didn't you realize that everyone has to agree to any work or duties they perform?

JIM. Like I said, that just doesn't work for us. Maybe with Emily's girls, but my daughter wouldn't do anything around the house at all if she could get away with just not "agreeing" to it!

BOB. No one really "gets away with anything" in Family Meetings, Jim, but I can understand your frustration in being out of control with your daughter. May I talk to you in more depth about the Family Meeting process? I think it might still work to help the situation with Sally.

JIM. Alright, go ahead.

BOB. Let's go back a little. Do you think we "bribe" children in Family Meetings?

JIM. Well, you give them money, don't you, for doing things at home like brushing their teeth, getting dressed, emptying the trash? Aren't these things they should do anyway? That's bribery in my book; what do you call it?

BOB. Would you allow them any allowance at all?

JIM. Sure, the kids need a little spending money, we do that. But what does that have to do with obeying what we say? Children are supposed to obey their parents.

BOB. Don't you get a salary at your job for what you do?

JIM. Come on! That's different, I make our living, that's my job!

BOB. But Jim, is it really different? Do you ever get a salary, out of the blue, with no work?

JIM. No, so what?

BOB. Isn't that what your allowance is like—like getting money out of the blue without earning it?

JIM. But they're kids! We have laws that say you can't force kids to work. Besides, I'm their father, not their employer.

BOB. True, our society intends to protect youngsters from abuse and exploitative labor. But, who says children shouldn't do reasonable work and self-maintenance, even at a young age? Don't you want to see your children earn their own way and value the effort it takes to make a living? How else will they learn to succeed out in the world?

JIM. Sure, but I'm not going to bribe them.

BOB. At what point or age should kids begin to learn to earn their way?

JIM. I don't know, teens, I guess. I don't like to see kids out working too young.

BOB. I'm not really talking about being "out" working in the world. Don't kids do things at home that are like work? And shouldn't they learn at an early age that you don't get the things you want in life without a proportional effort?

JIM. I suppose, but I still won't bribe them.

BOB. Jim, the Family Meeting no more bribes your children than your boss is bribing you when he pays you for a job well-done. Can you imagine what it would be like if your boss doled out a wad of cash every so often regardless of how you did your job? I don't think you'd respect your boss for long or feel like doing a particularly good job, would you? We all learn from and enjoy being rewarded for our efforts. Children need this too. Family Meetings are just an easier way to assist your children to take joy in working and earning step by step as they grow up.

JIM. Well, I'll think about what you've said about allowances as pay for certain jobs. We'll see. When I was a kid, what my dad said went, and nobody crossed him. When he told me to do something, I jumped, or hell, he'd thrash me raw. And believe me, I did what he said. The only meeting we had, if I got out of line, was a meeting with his belt. I may be old-fashioned, but what my father said was law. What was good enough for me in my family is good enough for my kid, and I damn well expect Sally to obey me as long as she's under eighteen.

BOB. You are entitled to your own views, Jim, but has it worked for you? Is it working with Sally, now?

JIM (*with an aggravated gesture*). . . No.

BOB. Family Meetings can't work overnight, Jim. It is most difficult to start meetings to solve an immediate crisis. I know you feel up against the ropes, Jim, with your daughter Sally gone and all. The first step is to acknowledge that what you are doing now isn't working. Could it be that there are some other things getting in the way of you and Sally getting along? Can you tell me what they might be?

JIM. What do you mean?

BOB. I mean, what if you *have* partially failed as a parent? Is it the end of the world? What's the worst case you might have to face with Sally?

JIM. Well, she's gone, I guess there isn't anything else that could happen. I just hate to see her get ground up by that world out there. That young kid that she's been hanging around with is probably getting into her pants, and then there's my brother-in-law . . . damn! I just can't stand it, I don't know how to explain it. I just wish she was my little Sally again. . . . (*What might have been tears are quickly suppressed and Jim sets his jaw tightly again.*)

BOB. It sounds like you love Sally, Jim, have you told her that lately?

JIM (*obviously moved and choked up, no reply*).

BOB. You're not alone in having a hard time getting your feelings out about Sally. Take your time, Jim. We'll come back to this in a while and take a closer look at how your daughter's becoming a sexual young woman has affected you and your relationship with her. Also let's take time to look at how jealousy and resentment have played into your relations with Sally. (*At this point Jim's beeper beeps and he leaves abruptly.*)

In subsequent sessions Jim discovered that deep down he was really jealous and resentful of his daughter's seemingly easy life and personal freedom. He got in touch with some deep resentment of his own father's harsh discipline. He also realized that a little part of him was secretly pleased when his father's heavy-handed approach did not work on his own daughter, Sally. It was almost as though he secretly wanted Sally to rebel when he treated her as his father had treated him. In this way he unconsciously made his father wrong.

After these insights, Jim was much more willing to give Family Meetings another try. He was even willing to use allowances and consensual agreements. He was skeptical, but said he would watch and see if it really worked.

Sally had lost a great deal of trust in her father, and it was some time before she would acknowledge that he was really trying to be more tolerant and flexible. Communication did improve between Sally and Jim, but this did not happen until Jim spent some time with Sally outside of Family Meetings. Jim and Sally did a few things together, just the two of them. He felt awkward, but pressed on to win Sally as a friend. He agreed, and so did Sally, to spend one evening a month together where they just did something they both enjoyed, without discussing family problems. As the years went by, Sally and Jim still had some major upsets, usually about boys and liberties. However, Jim helped Emily apply Family Meetings with her young girls. He did a commendable job and found that following the two cardinal rules of Family Meetings really did work!

The Big Wheel Incident

A little background may help you to understand this family better. Norman and Pam were in their late twenties. They had two children, Judy, age five, and Kevin, age nine. Judy was, for the most part, a sweet and happy child, although a little immature for her age. She went to kindergarten at a private Montessori school. Judy liked school a lot and regularly got good reports from her teachers. Kevin was in the fourth grade at one of the better elementary schools in the district. Kevin could be called an overactive but not strictly a hyperactive child. He had been taken to a psychiatrist for a short period several years before and had been given medication for a while. Initially, Kevin seemed to like seeing the doctor, but soon he became resistant. The effects seemed to be minimal, so his mother dropped the appointments.

Pam's primary responsibilities were at home, although she was taking two business courses at the local junior college. Norman had his own business which he had started as a small outlet for stereo and high fidelity components. For three years the family had lived in a modest house with a middle income life-style. Recently, Norman had expanded his business to sell personal computers and video equipment, and the family experienced a rather dramatic increase in affluence. They moved to a palatial abode in one of the more elite suburbs. Norman had employees, and it seemed necessary for him to be at work long hours and even on weekends. The younger child, Judy, had never really been a disciplinary problem, although she did have some trouble with stuttering. Kevin was another story. He had had a series of episodes at school over the past couple of years that had entailed a call from the vice principal to the parents. Fighting on the playground, pilfering from other kids' lunch boxes, and talking back to a teacher had occurred at one time or another. These incidents had been more frequent during the last year. Pam had tried to discipline Kevin at home, but she had a hard time getting him to obey consistently.

Kevin had gotten his way too many times because his mother was weary of carrying on the battle. Norman would give apparent support to Pam's disciplinary efforts. Things would build up for a long time, then Norman would warn Kevin to mind his mom and angrily spank him. On the other hand, Norman would often allow the children to do something Pam had forbidden for days or weeks. She thought Norman often undercut her authority with the kids. She sometimes felt her time was wasted in trying to keep control of Kevin. If Kevin had agreed with Pam to do chores on the weekend, Norman would as likely as not usurp this time and sweep Kevin off to go fishing or to the auto races. Things would build up between the parents. They would argue, then Norman would often spank young Kevin. Everything would go alright for a while. The family managed to survive from upset to upset by everyone more or less suppressing the whole business until the next upheaval with Kevin.

At this time, the family had tried Family Meetings about five times in three months. Initially there was a flurry of enthusiasm about Family Meetings. Pam had talked about meetings with much praise and with promises about how the kids would like them. The kids were thrilled by the expectation that they would all go to "Watersports," a local swimming complex with several immense water slides. The first few meetings went reasonably well, although Norman had to work and never made it to "Watersports." This family had so many activities that no Family Meeting occurred for some weeks. There were Judy's dancing lessons and swimming lessons. There were Kevin's piano lessons and daily baseball practice. Pam had recently become involved with "home parties," at which she sold kitchen products as well as franchises for others to sell these products. Norman had recently opened a second video computer store across town, and he had to make numerous trips to the new facility to get it off the ground.

These parents had good intentions about Family Meetings, but no time for them ever appeared on the horizon. Other things that just seemed to have to be done took the spotlight time after time. The few Family Meetings they did have always revolved around a mini-crisis with one of the kids. A rewarding activity was not planned to accompany each meeting. Generally, the kids got weekly allowances anyway, three dollars for Judy and eight for Kevin. Here is a glimpse of one such meeting.

Scene. Tuesday evening, Pam, Norman, Kevin, and Judy are seated at the dining room table. Yesterday, it is alleged, Kevin got mad at his little sister for bugging him, and he broke her Big Wheel. He's quiet and sullen. Judy is fidgity.

DAD . . . Okay, so we'll let Mommy keep notes this time. (pause) Kevin, sit up straight! You know this meeting is mostly for you. Now straighten up and pay attention!

MOM. Okay, please listen while I read the notes from our last meeting. (*Pam begins reading the last logged entry. It's been such a long time since the last meeting that not much in the notes is relevant to the present situation. After some discussion everyone agrees to think through*

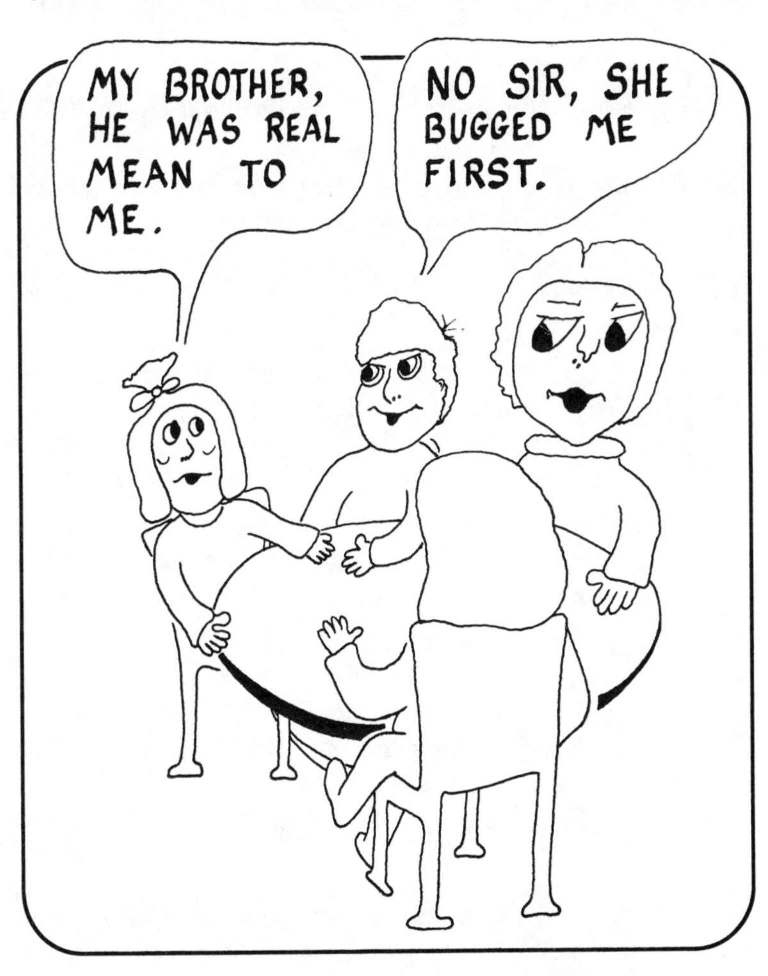

home jobs again and to essentially start fresh on that score. Pam now turns and asks Judy to tell about what happened between Kevin and her).

DAD. Wait, Kevin, let your sister tell her story and then you can have your turn. Go ahead, Judy, what happened?

JUDY. Well, . . . umm, I was playing and I wanted Kevin to push me on my Big Wheel. And I asked him nicely, but he was mean. . . .

KEVIN. No she didn't. She bugged me when I was working on my bike, then she hid my bicycle pump.

JUDY. No I didn't!

KEVIN. Yes, you did!

MOM. Stop it you guys! Judy, is there more you want to tell us?

JUDY. Well, . . . umm, next after that, my brother took my Big Wheel, without asking me, and he . . . and he rode it real, real hard and then he kicked it and broke the front wheel so it won't turn now. (*Judy starts to cry a little.*)

KEVIN. I told her not to bug me and she did anyway. The Big Wheel was cracked before. Anyway, I didn't break it. I just rode it a little ways and it just broke. Besides, Judy deserves it 'cause she was bugging me.

DAD. But it broke when you were using it, Kevin, so it was your responsibility. You know we've told you not to ride Judy's Big Wheel. You are too big for it. (*More discussion follows.*)

MOM. Kevin, you have admitted that the Big Wheel broke while you were playing with it. You know how much your sister loves her Big Wheel. Don't you think you should be the one to fix it?

KEVIN. No, 'cause she was bugging me and I didn't do anything.

MOM. What if we agree on some consequence for Judy if she bugs you? Would you be willing to take a conse-

quence for breaking the Big Wheel?

KEVIN (*looking down*). . . . I guess so.

MOM. Judy, what is something else you could do instead of following your brother around all the time? Maybe you and I could plan some things to do so that when you feel like pestering your brother you'll come to me first and then do something else.

JUDY. Okay.

MOM. Kevin, what would be fair about the Big Wheel?

KEVIN (*almost whispering while pulling his hand along the table edge*) . . . I don't know.

DAD. I think you ought to fix the tricycle, son, and be docked a dollar next week if you fail. What do you think?

KEVIN (*silent, looks down*).

MOM. We aren't going to finish our meeting until we get this business taken care of. So make up your mind, Kevin, what will it be?

KEVIN. Oh, alright, I'll fix the Big Wheel, but I think Judy should have to go to her room if she bugs me.

DAD. Judy, will you agree to go to your room if your mom thinks you are bothering your brother?

JUDY. Yeah. (*She squirms around in her chair.*)

DAD (*wanting to get the meeting done with*) . . . Okay, what else is there to talk about? (*There is a little more discussion before the meeting breaks up until the next week.*)

The family interactions run smoothly the rest of the evening. By Thursday the old ways have returned. Kevin is ignoring his sister. She still bugs him. They quarrel. Pam is busy and doesn't intervene very often, but does send Judy to her room once when things get out of hand. Pam notices that, as the week goes by, Kevin makes no move to repair the Big Wheel. She waits until the next Tuesday evening meeting to raise the subject with Kevin. Tuesday comes and Norman has to work late at the new store, but Pam and the kids have a meeting anyway. Pam agrees to keep the notes again. She reads last week's minutes, including the consequence regarding the Big Wheel incident.

MOM. Kevin, did you fix your sister's tricycle as you promised?

KEVIN (*long silence*) . . . No.

MOM. Why not?

KEVIN. I forgot.

JUDY. That doesn't count, Kevin, you promised!

KEVIN. You bugged me all week, so I don't have to fix your old Big Wheel.

MOM. Kevin, do you understand that you lose a dollar from your allowance?

KEVIN. That's not fair, she bugged me and you didn't stop her.

MOM. But, Kevin, you know that you agreed to give up a dollar if you didn't fix the Big Wheel by tonight. And you know that was the agreement no matter how your sister behaved.

KEVIN. Take the dollar, I don't care.

MOM. Kevin, you know you're really asking for it. How would it be if we took all your allowance away?

KEVIN. I don't care. Dad'll give me money anyway. You can't make me do anything. (*At this point Kevin gets up from the table and storms into his room and slams the door.*)

Although Pam wanted very much for Norman to take a hand in this matter, he was just too busy at the stores to have time to deal with Kevin that week. Two more weeks slipped by. As Kevin began to have more physical fights with his sister, Pam became somewhat alarmed and asked me what to do.

After I consuted a couple of times with just the parents, they decided to change several aspects of their Family Meetings. Norman began to realize some of the truth in the saying,

"NO SUCCESS IN THE WORLD IS WORTH FAILURE AT HOME."

It's easy to intellectualize about how you ought to spend more time with your kids. Fortunately for this family, this father was willing to go the second mile and actually spend more time, and more consistent time, with his kids. He was slower to perceive how his rescuing Kevin from Pam's attempts at consistent discipline only made matters worse. In time, Norman began to discern that he was, in effect, attempting to "buy" his children's respect and affection. There was also an element of anger toward Pam, stemming from his feeling that she was not giving him enough attention. Meanwhile, his recent upsurgence of affluence had pumped up his ego and brought out a streak of selfishness. Like Kevin, Norman usually got his way, especially in the material world. Pam knew that she needed to make a special effort to be more regular and consistent with the kids. She acknowledged resenting Norm for always, "skimming the cream with the kids and never being around for the hard work."

After some mutual release of pent-up emotions, this couple decided to revamp their Family Meeting practices in the following ways:

1) They agreed to start meetings without accusations and intimidation. Norman agreed not to begin with phrases like, "You know this meeting is mostly for you."
2) They decided to set up regular rewards for cheerful attendance of Family Meetings. They arranged first to inquire of the children as to what they would really like to do during or just after a meeting.
3) Norman decided not to initiate suggestions of particular consequences, as he had with Kevin about the Big Wheel, until the children had ample time to come up with their own ideas.
4) They decided to redouble their efforts to keep Family Meetings positive. They would avoid emotional issues until good attitudes about meetings had been stabilized. They planned a gradual transition of power from parents to the consensual family. They set for themselves the goal of having true family sovereignty within the next twelve meetings.
5) Both parents agreed to be even more aware of their roles. Particularly, they would restrain from rail-

roading the children over any decisions, such as Pam had done meeting before last when she told Kevin they wouldn't end the meeting until he made up his mind about the Big Wheel issue.

6) They concluded that the children's allowances were extremely high. Norman acknowledged some degree of ego gratification on his part for lavishing money upon his children. If allowances were to be earnings or an incentive for good conduct, surprise gifts and pocket cash must be more contingent upon right behavior. They decided that rather than suddenly and arbitrarily cutting allowances, they would take it before the children in positive form, asking each youngster first to list appropriate chores for the week, and then to suggest an amount for each job well done. The total allowance would be built from the ground up. Rather than being docked for failure, the children would be rewarded for success.

7) Finally, they heartily agreed that Family Meetings needed to be more fun for the parents, too. They chose to discuss this with the children at the next meeting.

The expectation of these parents changed with regard to meetings. They had more of a long-range perspective now. It seemed evident that the Big Wheel incident would have to wait. It snagged Pam emotionally that Kevin appeared to be getting away with misbehavior. But Pam felt some hope that at least they would be better able to put an end to any future Big Wheel incidents. When Pam and Norman got home, they asked Judy and Kevin if they would have a short meeting, just to discuss Family Meetings and fun projects. At this meeting they would not discuss punishment or wrongdoing. The kids agreed. Kevin said he would lead the meeting and take notes, if they didn't have to go back over the last meeting's notes.

KEVIN (*With evident pride at being chairperson*). Okay, does anyone have anything to say?

MOM. Yes, I do. I would like us to discuss some things we can do together that we all enjoy. What are your ideas (*gesturing around the table*)?

JUDY. I want to go to Fun Town (*a giant amusement park in a nearby city*).

DAD. Kevin, will you write that in our family notebook? Since that's a big trip, maybe we should save Fun Town until we have had a bunch of good meetings.

JUDY. How many meetings, Daddy?

MOM. Well, how about if we travel to Fun Town after we have ten good meetings?

KEVIN. Okay, but I want to stay a whole week. We never get long vacations. Please can we stay a week?

DAD. I don't know, Kevin, I can't leave work that long . . . maybe your mom could stay longer with you kids.

MOM. Norm! Don't you dare! You agreed to put the family first and you know that you haven't been away from work for a whole week since I can remember. I'll talk to you about this later . . . Okay, what are some things we can enjoy closer to home?

KEVIN. I want to go to a motocross.

MOM. But, do we all enjoy dirt bikes? Let's try right now to stick to things that everyone of us is sure to enjoy. How about if we go ice skating or to the zoo? (*Everyone nods approval.*) Let's see if we can pick just two things we all like, one for tonight and one for after our next Family Meeting.

DAD (*now that the kids have made at least one suggestion*). I brought home a brand new video game that we can all play. It's called "Space Adventurers." How about if we play that today, and if it's nice next week, let's go to the big park and take our frisbees and kites and have a picnic?

KEVIN. Okay, I like that, but Dad, do you promise that you will really go with us to the park?

Dad. I promise, Kevin, but we'll have to do it Sunday afternoon. (*Kevin goes around the table and asks each person individually and then writes in the notebook.*)

Mom. I think we've got some good ideas now. How about if we end this meeting now and play the video game? We'll have time to talk about other things next week. (*They all agree, and Dad goes into his study to get the video cartridge he promised. Before long everyone is caught up in "Space Adventurers."*)

Kevin and Judy continued to have their conflicts during the following week, although with less intensity. At the next Family Meeting it was Judy's turn to lead. She printed the date, her name as leader, and the names of everyone there. Mom then took notes and assisted Judy in leading the meeting.

Judy. Umm, does anyone have anything to say?

Kevin. Could I have my allowance? I didn't get any last week. (*Until recently he hadn't even noticed.*)

Mom. Judy, why don't you ask everyone what they should do for allowances each week?

Judy (*wiggling about and making faces*). Okay, Kevin, what should you do?

Kevin. I don't see why I have to do chores for allowance. Johnny (*a neighborhood friend*) gets almost as much allowance as I do and he doesn't have to do "chores." (*Kevin made the word sound funny and Judy started to giggle, but she stopped when Mom reminded her that she was leading the Family Meeting.*)

Dad. Remember, Johnny lives in a different family, maybe they have different rules for him. Are you sure Johnny doesn't have to do things around the house? I think I saw him out mowing the lawn just this weekend.

Kevin. Johnny doesn't have to mow the lawn, he just likes to do that sometimes.

Mom. Kevin, are there some things around here that

you like to do? Don't you enjoy watering sometimes and feeding Hefty (*the family dog*)?

KEVIN. Not really. (*He shifts his attention to slipping his belt buckle in and out of a belt loop.*)

JUDY. I like to do some things around the house.

DAD. What are they Judy?

JUDY. Ummm, umm, I like to feed the fish, I like to run the vacuum, and I like to set the table.

MOM (*now that she better understands the importance of participating as a peer*). . . . I like to fold the clothes, I usually enjoy cooking, I like helping you guys with dancing and piano. . . . (*Now, Dad chimes in.*)

DAD. I like earning a living so I can provide you all with a nice home and nice things, I like painting and repairing things around here. Just think, Kevin, many of the things you like couldn't happen if I didn't like my "chores." (*Dad made a funny sound with "chores," mimicking Kevin. Judy giggles, then everyone begins to laugh.*)

MOM. A family really can't enjoy life much if everyone doesn't pitch in. Kevin, is there anything you like doing for other members of our family? I remember times when you seemed to enjoy playing with your sister and helping care for the pets.

KEVIN. Well, sometimes, maybe.

DAD. Kevin, would it be fair to earn allowance according to how much you do your share of family work?

KEVIN. Well, I do want to do some things for the family but I hate sweeping the garage and scooping up after Hefty.

DAD. We're mostly interested in what you are willing to do for allowance, forget what you hate right now. Will you make a list of things you are agreeable to do and how much you think you should earn for each one? Maybe we can trade some jobs you don't like for ones you

like better. Remember, we all have some things to do that we don't like completely.

KEVIN. Oh, okay, I'll make a list. (*Mom gives him a pat on the shoulder.*)

MOM. Judy, I'll help you make your list so we can talk about it at our next Family Meeting. Why don't you check with everyone now and see if it's time to close the meeting for today?

JUDY. Umm, does anyone have more to talk about?

KEVIN. Yeah. What about my allowance for this week?

JUDY. Mommy, what about my brother's allowance for this week?

MOM. It's okay dear, I heard your brother. Since you don't have your list yet, let's talk about just what you need money for this week. What are your "needs" but not your "greeds"?

KEVIN. What do you mean, "needs," "greeds"? (*He and Judy laugh.*)

DAD. You know, what's important, not just extra baggage?

Kevin mentions school lunch money, snacks, and a few incidentals. They ask him how much money this amounts to, and after further discussion they arrive at six dollars per week for Kevin and one dollar for Judy. They talk further about sharing family responsibilities and the good feelings that come from doing a job well. They agree to talk about regular earnings the next week. The meeting ends peacefully and they head for the big park, picnic in hand.

During the week Norman grumbled to Pam about Kevin's self-centeredness, but they agreed to continue open discussions at the Family Meetings and not to upturn the process by unilateral parental discipline. Pam was basically pleased with their smidgen of progress. She began to realize that an important side benefit was emerging: She and Norman began feeling better about each other!

At the next meeting there was a constructive discussion about what we "get by giving." Kevin submitted a short list of household duties and through much negotiating he accepted a total of $5.65 as his weekly allowance. They shifted the focus to what he would do the following week, rather than what he had failed to do. He agreed to his list partly because he left off several distasteful "chores." In trade, he would receive less money, but the tasks he was assigned were more likely to be completed acceptably. They all agreed that Kevin had managed to take most of the Family Meeting energy for the past two weeks and that it would be Judy's turn for some extra attention next week.

The Glass Window

Carol and Gene had good success with Family Meetings and had been holding them more or less regularly for several years by the time the window incident took place. Their boys were about eight and ten at that time. In the past, this family had many adjustments to make. Carol had suffered through a difficult divorce. The biological father visited often and sometimes intrusively. There was an admixture of muddy confusion and bright new hopes.

Gene, Carol's second husband, was poorly equipped for an "instant" family. He had been slow, and, at times, most resistant to his new role as surrogate father. He was primarily involved with his relationship to Carol, and he found himself resenting the boys' demands on their mother's time. Uncomfortable feelings more often arose between Gene and the younger boy, Ronnie, who was very attached to his mom and who was least able to comprehend the role of this new person on the scene. Although Gene filled many of the roles of father, he got little acknowledgement. The boys' genetic father would scurry the boys off for adventurous weekends and return them on Sunday night at the end of his visitation period. The boys were typically bedraggled and worn out. Carol and Gene would labor for the first few days of each week to get the boys back into their home routine. There was often little time for family enjoyment during week days or school days, and before long the biological father's visitation cycle would begin again. During the early years there was much enmity and little cooperation between the boys' biological parents. This served to keep the family nearly always on edge. With considerable support from Carol, Gene proposed Family Meetings when the boys were about four and six. After some fairly typical struggles in early sessions, Family Meetings evolved into a stabilizing and ameliorating force in an often stressful family environment. Carol's older boy, Bruce, tended to be contemplative and serious. Ronnie was more frequently a disciplinary problem. Family Meetings proved a great service in providing balance and fairness in all matters pertaining to the boys.

After about two years of Family Meetings, Ronnie and Bruce had become very efficient in using the process. Resistances to coming to Family Meetings were nearly gone because meetings could be brief and to the point. Enjoyable and instructive discussions were more likely to emerge now that Family Meeting procedures were established and taken for granted. By now, each family member trusted the process and had developed a businesslike attitude toward solving problems within a meeting. Consequences had become more matter-of-fact and could be carried out without a loss of dignity. Long practice had conditioned family habits so that a real sense of teamwork was experienced at meetings. Of course there were still problems; Ronnie in particular had numerous slippages of accountability for his actions. Consequences were frequent enough for Ronnie that sometimes the family had to just wipe the slate clean of back issues concerning him so that meetings could continue without becoming too much of a courtroom. Nonetheless, consistency of follow-up with Ronnie was still considerably greater than it would have been without Family Meetings.

Gene's relations with the boys were observably improved to the point that tolerant and even warm feelings prevailed most of the time among Gene, Ronnie, and Bruce. Gene still kept a certain distance from the boys, but Family Meetings worked to draw them together more and more. Often the boys would be the ones to ask for a Family Meeting. On their own, Ronnie and Bruce had started individual notebooks or journals wherein they kept track of their various jobs, agreements, and wants. For example, Ronnie very much wanted a pet rabbit. Rather than creating a lot of dead air time and vocalized pauses at meetings, the boys would typically pull out their notepads at a meeting immediately and proceed to enumerate their activities and accomplishments for the week. Bonuses were often in order for jobs well done. By the time the boys were eight and ten, they had developed wholesome independence in their thinking and were nearly entirely self-maintaining in the practicalities of daily living. The boys learned the technique of follow-up so well that they would follow up on things Mom or Gene might have forgotten.

Scene. It was mid-week when Ronnie, now eight years old, came running into the house announcing that "we need to have an emergency Family Meeting right away." The whole family happened to be home that afternoon, so rather than asking Ronnie what he was so big-eyed and breathless about, they just went ahead and had a meeting.

RONNIE. Something awful happened that I sorta did, but I didn't mean to.

BRUCE (*almost laughing*). . . . Goll-y, Ron what did you do?

RONNIE. Well . . . , I was playing baseball with Chrissy (*a neighbor girl*) and, well, I was at bat and she threw the ball really, really hard. I bunted it but it went by mistake into the Caldarone's living room.

MOM (*With raised eyebrows*). You mean through their plate glass window?

RONNIE. Honest, it was an accident ... (*he was obviously shaken by what must have seemed a great catastrophe*).

GENE. Well ... okay, what would be fair in this situation?

RONNIE (*shifts into thinking for a moment*). ... I think I should pay for the window out of my allowance, and tell the Caldarone's I'm sorry ... and I'll give up playing with Chrissy for two weeks.

It was a shock to everyone else at the table to hear Ronnie voluntarily give himself all these consequences. Since Ronnie was not usually so cooperative about reaping what he had sown, Gene became a little suspicious that there was more to the incident or perhaps more damage. Gene suggested that first Ronnie go over to the neighbors and apologize, and then find out the cost of the damage. The meeting was put on hold for a few minutes while Ronnie ran back over to "the scene of the crime." Meanwhile, Carol called Mrs. Caldarone to assure her that the shattered window would be promptly replaced. Soon, Ronnie came running back in, breathless but relieved, even excited. He had the offending softball in his hand. Fortunately for all concerned, the damage was just as Ronnie had reported it and the Caldarones had insurance that would pay for most of the repairs.

Sometimes you can see your children's deeper values and commitments in bold relief during a crisis situation. Admittedly, this was a minor crisis to everyone but Ronnie. It delighted both Gene and Carol immensely that when tested, Ronnie came through with flying colors. It makes Family Meetings downright enjoyable for parents when their job is to increase allowances for exceptional work or reduce consequences because a youngster has become overzealous in penalizing himself. This was such a case. Ronnie dearly loved to play with the little neighbor girl, Chrissy. He could barely stand not seeing her for even one day, much less two weeks. His willingness to pay for the window was admirable, and sums were

deducted from his allowance for that purpose. But Ronnie could not get family consensus for his other consequences. He asked for agreement on his self-generated idea about Chrissy but received no votes. Even his brother would not condone his request. "Why?" he asked;

and it was a real pleasure to inform him that he was being too hard on himself. This meeting ended on a happy note. Ronnie was relieved to have even fewer consequences than he had asked for. Everyone else was pleased that he had taken substantial consequences so cheerfully. They strongly praised Ron for his honesty and eagerness to right his error. He got to play with Chrissy after all, and he agreeably moved his baseball diamond.

THE FAMILY MEETING NOTEBOOK

Your family notebook can be as elaborate or as simple as you like. It can be a family record, scrapbook, a creative project; or, it can simply include the date, the names of those present, the name of the note-taker, and a brief statement of family decisions and agreements. Keeping a regular and up-to-date family log will add cohesion and continuity to your meetings. Your notes are the chain of words that link meetings together. Don't lose them. Like any minutes of a meeting, Family Meeting notes can be tedious and mundane. Keep them anyway. They will become more precious to you with each succeeding meeting. Store them in a safe place that all family members know about. It never hurts to make a photocopy to keep in a separate location as a backup. A good habit is to read the notes for a Family Meeting at the end of the meeting to confirm that everyone agrees on the wording while decisions are still fresh in everyone's mind. ***Sometimes, for very important family agreements, it helps to have every family member sign or initial the notes before the meeting ends.***

Your journal is the tangible account of the promises you have made to each other. It is the repository of family contracts and covenants. It is the record of the court and the family law book. It is the baseline from which you can view each family member's progress and setbacks. It is the history book of the love and patience you have shown one another.

In order to get a sense of Family Meetings over the longer run, an extended excerpt from a family notebook is presented below. Most of the previous examples have focused on early Family Meetings, on starting them and learning the process. The notes below are taken from the notebook of a family that held meetings for over a year and that has continued on for many more. The entries that follow span six months of Family Meetings. Every family is different and each family log is unique. The portion revealed below is meant only to serve as an illustration to give you perspective on the process. It's not necessary to follow this model in either form or content. The names and certain facts have been changed to safeguard the privacy of those involved.

Context:

This family lived in a rural setting with orchards and farming nearby. Gayle and Bill were in their early thirties and had two boys. Daniel was seven years old at this time. His brother, Michael, was almost nine. They were in the second and fourth grades, respectively. These children had learned the Family Meeting procedures. They enjoyed leading meetings and taking notes. They took consequences fairly well and usually didn't conceive of consequences as "punishment." They earned allowances through Family Meetings as well as privileges and other intangible rewards. They trusted Family Meeting agreements and usually liked meetings. There were still occasions when it was very difficult to get everyone together for a particular meeting. Regularity wasn't always observed, yet meetings had become efficient despite skipping sessions for several weeks at a time.

In this family each child had decided some time ago to keep his own separate notebook of personal and family business. Both youngsters brought their notebooks to meetings, took notes, and referred to them when asked about their jobs for the past week. This family had agreed that most of the time Gayle or Bill would keep the "official" Family Meeting notes. After the last week's notes were reviewed, these boys usually took turns telling what their agreements were for the past week. They told what jobs they had done and estimated what each felt he had earned justly as his allowance. There was time for talk, feedback, and then final negotiation for the amount everyone could agree on. After this initial business was handled concerning allowances and follow-up from the last week, the meeting was open for anyone to share feelings and to talk about anything that concerned a family member. At the point where we look in on their meeting log, seven-year-old Daniel had been working on "remembering" his promises and agreements from day to day without being reminded.

Daniel (*age 7*), Michael (*age 9*), Gayle (*Mom, age 32*), Bill (*Dad, age 31*)

January 7

Gayle keeps notes. All present. Go over minutes. Daniel reviews his doings for the week: set table, do juice, put tools away, feed Samantha [dog], bed on time. All agree he's done a much better job this week in remembering his agreements. Allowance will include ten-cent bonus. Michael tells what he has done for week: set table, juice oranges, water gardens, clean room, clean bathroom, garbage, compost, sweep, fold clothes. All okay. He also earns a ten-cent bonus. Allowances: Daniel, 60 cents; Michael, 80 cents. Michael suggests that Daniel help with the compost. Mom will go to lumberyard and buy timber and scraps for boys' projects. She will also go to bank. Boys agree be more quiet in house, no stomping! Michael has good attitude. Daniel asks what "attitude" means.

January 14 [no meeting]

January 21 [no meeting]

January 28

Bill keeps notes. All here. Review notes. Daniel slipped up on cleaning room; all else okay. Allowances: Daniel, 35 cents; Michael, 60. All agree. Boys will at bedtime: a) put on pj's, b) brush teeth, c) clean room so it's neat and orderly, d) put out clothes for school, e) be in bed by 8:30. After school they will, a) change clothes, b) put away coats and school clothes, c) clean lunch pail without being asked. Agreed. "Alone time" at 6:30 p.m. each day we will set aside twenty minutes of quiet time when everyone will think good thoughts. Boys agree, NO DILLY-DALLYING when asked to do something. Gayle asks Michael what a "walking mantra" is. He says it's a word of wisdom or a good thought that he says to himself or aloud while walking or doing any activity. Daniel asks if Mom will do clothes, etc., ahead of time so he will not be late getting ready for school. Gayle agrees. Michael says, "Mom didn't go to lumberyard, please this week?" Agreed. Also, he asks for a family outing after next Family Meeting. Discussion. Decide to go to planetarium one week from today.

February 4

Bill on notes. All present. Review last notes. Everyone agrees this has been a better week! Congratulations to Daniel for mending his own bedspread. Daniel, 55 cents; Michael, 75. Daniel reminds Mommy about wood again. Michael asks if he can play drop ball Saturday in place of helping Dad with firewood. Agreed. Boys feel that if they carry in firewood they should get to stay up for the fire. All agree. Everyone excited about going to planetarium today.

February 11

Gayle takes notes. All present. Review last notes. Everyone agrees planetarium laser show was wonderful. Still aren't going to bed as agreed without our asking. Daniel, 40 cents; Michael, 65. Remind Michael to clean eyeglasses. Daniel agrees he won't throw or kick objects into air in living room or other "dangerous" places. Mommy gets big hug for getting wood. But Daniel wants balsa wood! We agree that Michael can substitute two books on Cub Scout list. Daniel promises to be good when we ask. He will decide (on his own) to stop being silly at wrong times.

February 18 [no meeting]

February 25 [no meeting]

March 4

Daniel takes notes with Mom's help. All present. Review. Daniel, 40 cents; Michael, 70. Agree, same allowances for missed weeks too. Mom and Dad promise to try to be happier and not argue. My brother needs a model boat and glue for Cub Scouts. My brother agrees to take a consequence for yelling and hitting. My brother, he will do laundry Monday as consequence. Everyone agrees to pay more attention at Family Meetings. My brother still sick with cough.

March 11 [no meeting]

March 18 [no meeting]

March 25

Daniel prints notes with Dad's help. All here. Me and my brother were good for getting up and doing our jobs without being asked. We were late getting to bed. Daniel, 45 cents; Michael 65. We will try to be more quiet. My brother needs boat cement. Mom and Dad need to talk about budget.

April 1
Michael takes notes. No Family Meeting, April FOOLS! Allowances are 70 cents for Michael and 50 for Dan; the same for each previous week we missed. Agreed. Dan and I will come home no later than fifteen 'til six each evening. I still need boat cement! Dan promises not to threaten violence. Everyone agrees not to yell at him.

April 8
Gayle takes notes. Everyone present. Go over previous week. The boys review activities for week, no

problem agreeing on fairness of allowances, Daniel, 40 cents; Michael, 65. Daniel having trouble with Ellie, [neighbor girl, age four]. We encourage him to do something good back to her when she does something mean to him. Michael asks if he can bring his new baseball mitt to school. Okay for a one day trial. Michael still wants boat cement.

April 15 [no meeting]

April 22

Bill keeps notes. All here. Review. Daniel, 35 cents; Michael, 70; agreed. Daniel agrees to try to be more serious. Michael got cement, hurrah! Boys will do orange juice, remember to use cold water for cleaning bowls. Did Daniel do compost? Yes. Daniel sassed his mom three times this week. Michael thinks he should be punished by not being allowed to go over to Sara's to play today. Daniel is a space case today, first he said he shouldn't be punished, then he said he should be spanked, then he changed his mind. Gayle thinks he should take a consequence, maybe something other than being kept home from Sara's. Most of all she wants NO MORE SASSING! Discussion. Daniel finally suggests that he will clean the front bath and thoroughly. Apologizes to his mom and agrees that if he sasses again this week he won't be able to have Sara over next week as planned.

April 29

Bill keeps notes. Daniel won't agree to meeting. Bad feelings. Kids seem tired and cranky from outing yesterday.

May 6 [no meeting]

May 13

Bill's notes. All here. Review notes. Discussion of past two weeks and missed meetings. Boys agree to 35 and 65 cents for each week of missed allowances. Daniel wants to earn more allowance. Michael reminds Dan that it was his choice to do less than Michael each week *and* to get less allowance. Discussion of what Daniel can do to earn more money. He thinks about it and decides to stick with his old jobs and old allowance. We remind him that at any time he can do more and earn more. Boys will be more careful brandishing yardsticks! Remember to take quiet time at 6:30 p.m. each day and reflect on good experiences during the day.

Think of blessings for day. Daniel wants two chickens and a rooster. All agree he must be agreeable and cooperative for two consecutive weeks then we will buy him some chicks.

May 20

Gayle is notekeeper. All here. Minutes of last meeting. Allowances, Daniel 35, Michael 60 cents. Michael lied about eating Dad's sandwich. He tells truth and all forgiven. Boys agree to be quieter in mornings, especially in bathroom! Remember to save boxes for apples. Michael wants a home fire drill. Discuss disaster preparedness. Vote about keeping cat. Yes. Decide to name her Tabby. Discuss family outing.

May 27

Bill notekeeper. All present. Review. Weather hot! Daniel had some difficulty remembering his chores. He suggests 25 cents; we agree; 65 cents for Michael. Daniel will wind hose MWF, and will water his and Michael's garden every night this week.

Michael will water every plant in the front. Michael threatened Daniel with knife; agree he will not get his pocket knives back until July 8. Michael promises never to do this again.

[Michael signs his name here.]

Daniel volunteers that he didn't play fair with Michael at cards, and he lied and stole some candy from his brother. He says he won't steal anymore, and he will tell the truth.

[Daniel signs his name here.]

Daniel agrees that he hasn't been cooperative enough to have earned the chickens. He will check back in three weeks.

June 4

Bill notekeeper. All here. Boys used motel shuffleboard without permission. Meeting aborted—very hot weather, everyone grumpy.

June 11 [no meeting]

June 18 [no meeting]

June 24

Bill notekeeper. All here. Minutes reviewed. Allowances, repeat last allowance for missed weeks. This week Daniel, 30 cents, Michael, 75 cents. Agreed. Discussion of play with knives and safety. All agree to these rules: 1) point knife down, 2) hand to a person with it pointing away, 3) never run with knife, 4) cut away from yourself, 5) never throw knives.

[Everyone signs notes here.]

Michael acknowledged for being good during hard times! Daniel good job feeding Tabby, watering, and cleaning; still too silly at wrong times. Tabby must be fixed! Discuss summer schedule. Mom and Dad want an hour each day to read or write. Michael wants to play baseball, work with leather. Discuss angry feelings and how to handle. Agree to get a punching clown to set up in garage. Punch it when mad, not each other! Discussion of TV watching. Agree to take friend's suggestion and pick TV shows for the coming week at the Family Meeting. Watch *only* the shows selected. All agree. Gayle and I offer the boys a prize if they memorize some brief and worthwhile sayings, 25–35 words. They like the idea.

Comments:

Much of the discussion that goes on in a Family Meeting may not show up in your family notebook. Your minutes will contain only what your family takes the pains to include. You may not write much, but pause to consider that what you do write down are those things you all could and did in fact agree upon. What an accomplishment! Your notebook should at least contain decisions, if not discussions. It is really important that you log the name and request of any family member during a meeting regardless of how silly the request might seem to the note-taker. In this way, each child is acknowledged for their input, however insignificant it might appear. Kids feel good when they see their ideas and suggestions written down in the family record. For some families, tape recording or videotaping an occasional meeting may prove interesting. If you have an easel, you may want to take family notes on the big sheets that everyone can see at once. Kids love this approach, which also facilitates the sense of Family Meetings as educational.

An easel or chalk board is especially useful if a portion of your Family Meeting is run as a "brainstorm." In a "brainstorm" all participants offer their ideas, which are then taken down or tape recorded without any censure or analysis. Whether an idea is good or bad doesn't matter at that point. Once everyone has had a chance to share, then and only then is it time to begin discussion, critiques, and the setting of priorities. Brainstorming is especially useful when you're trying to find good and appropriate consequences. If some portion of your meeting time is spent this way, you are more likely to take a matter-of-fact approach to all issues and the meeting will run on a more even keel.

Follow-up, like brainstorming, is an important aspect of Family Meetings. You can see that the family above in the notebook excerpts preferred to get the more difficult matters, like follow-up and consequences, over with first. This left the remainder of their meetings less tense and more likely to be fun and lighthearted for everyone. If you institute follow-up as a regular habit in your meetings, there will be little mileage in trying to "get away" with anything. This has an excellent effect on children: they become very self-regulating. A healthy conscience develops and children are more likely to be honest and open about their errors of judgment and wrong behavior. Notice that, in the example, Daniel *volunteered* that he stole and didn't play fair. What a joy and relief to parents when they can begin to trust their children's moral integrity!

Follow-up also keeps parents accountable. Michael first asked his parents for boat cement on March 4. He asked again on March 25, and April 1. No glue had shown by April 8, then finally the patient lad got his cement as recorded on April 22, eight weeks later. Follow-up may be slow, but it can be sure. How about the case of the lumber for projects? Parents have to keep promises too. Daniel asked for wood on January 7 and eventually got it February 11. The delay was not a consequence. It's just that parents are human, too. After all of Daniel's waiting for the wood, it wasn't what he wanted. It wasn't balsa wood. Here was a great opportunity for a family argument. The notes treat the wrong wood incident as just another fact. Perhaps the Family Meeting procedures helped Gayle to avoid bad feelings with Daniel, especially since she made a big effort that Dan may not have appreciated.

You may have noticed, in the example, that Bill and Gayle must have been having some squabbles of their own just before March 4. Daniel wrote in the family log book that his parents agreed to be happier and not argue. To receive honest criticism and even take consequences for broken agreements is a humbling experience that sincere parents will value. One way to facilitate objective feedback from your youngsters is to make meetings a safe place for such risks. Welcome "good cheer comments" from your children. "Good cheer comments" are criticisms conveyed in a friendly and caring tone. Somehow it's a lot easier to receive criticism when the person criticizing isn't angry and has your best interests at heart. "Good cheer comments" are the ideal way to let your kids know that they have fallen down on their agreements. There is much less reason to get mad, since in the long run the Family Meeting procedures will take care of the offending conduct. Parents are freer to love their children with unconditional love.

Did the weekly allowances for Michael and Daniel seem low? Every family has its own economic realities to contend with. The example above shows that allowances need not be lavish to be effective. If you follow the principle of meeting the children's "needs" and not their "greeds," this will help define the appropriate allowance for each child. Generally, children like to please their parents because they love and respect them. Do you remember folding clothes for your mom or helping your dad with the car when you were young? And just for the sheer delight of helping? If this side of children is to be brought out through Family Meetings, "earning" must be a positive part of living in a family. Money cannot love, but you can both love your children and demystify money through Family Meetings as earning becomes a natural and normal way to be on the family team. Rewards are earned and contingent upon right behavior. Soon kids take earning their way for granted. Work along with play becomes a way of life, not a burden to be constantly resisted and resented. Kids who earn their way grow up with self-respect. Later on in life they take work and jobs in stride.

Even though many meetings were missed in the example, the family agreements ran relatively smoothly. Out of a possible twenty-eight meetings in six months, this family missed ten and aborted two. They missed almost half their meetings; yet, with the family notebook and some efforts, a thread of continuity was maintained and, overall, the process worked admirably.

HINTS AND SUGGESTIONS

Open the World to Your Children

One of the greatest frustrations of childhood is being told "no." Some parents seem to say "no" or "don't" all the time. Others never seem to say "no" at all. The marvel is that both sets of parents probably believe sincerely in what they are doing. Family Meetings can tremendously reduce the number of times you have to say "no" to your children. At the same time, unsafe or objectionable conduct will be dropping away meeting by meeting. Self-discipline gradually intervenes in those situations where a "no" would have formerly been required. YOU CAN ALWAYS SAY "YES" TO YOUR CHILDREN, with whatever qualifications your family agrees upon. What an elevation in mood parents feel when they are relieved of having to say "no," "don't," and "stop" so much of the time. Recall the case of Secret Fire where the youngsters were first told "no" about playing with matches, then in a Family Meeting they were told "yes," but with qualifications. The youngsters had to have an adult present and follow the fire safety rules, but "yes" prevailed. Many times children will think through their own requests and realize that the best answer is "no." For parents whose children constantly ask for things or liberties, the experience of being nagged and having to say "no" can be nearly eliminated with Family Meetings. When time is not of the essence, children can be reminded to wait until the Family Meeting to bring up their "want" or question.

With patience, this practice of waiting can be established to whatever degree you desire, so that children come to expect that their wants will be fairly handled at Family Meetings and not necessarily on the spur of the moment. In the family notebook illustration, Daniel and

Michael even learned to keep their own notes of issues they might want to bring up at a Family Meeting. Children learn to accept deferred goals more easily when they have the assurance that their concerns will be heard and acted on fairly, even though it may take a long time. The ability to await long term goals cheerfully and to defer fulfillment must be at the heart of the ability as humans to show patience, tact, and tolerance. What an advantage to your children to be able to prepare for these character traits in their formative years.

One family opened the world to their children by essentially saying that the kids could have whatever they wanted—"anything in the world"—provided there was agreement in the Family Meeting. Very soon their eight-year-old son, David, brought to a Family Meeting some literature on motorcycles for kids. The parents were surprised to find that unlicensed youngsters can ride motor driven cycles off the public roads, for instance, on a family's private property. The brochures were given to David by some neighbors who were dirt-bike enthusiasts. David tested out the new "open world" Family Meeting rule by asking if he could have a small motorcycle if he earned the money himself. His parents were taken aback even more when he brought out over fifty dollars he had meticulously saved from many months of allowances. His parents had not realized that he could have saved so much, but it was true. They were alarmed as it dawned on them that David was quite intent on his motorcycle mission. These parents knew a friend who had suffered brain damage from a motorcycle accident; they were not minded to let David have a cycle under any circumstances. I urged them to go through with the Family Meeting process anyway. I reminded them that their Family Meeting vote was just as powerful as their kids'. They could block any family decision they wanted, including this one. ***Parents should not hesitate absolutely to veto a family decision if their wiser judgment tells them to do so.*** Use this power sparingly; compromise if possible.

This family spent two meetings on the discussion of motorcycles, safety, know-how, fuel, insurance, and numerous styles, colors, and prices. It was finally agreed that David could have a motorcycle. David agreed to a long list of requirements including skills to be learned, money to be earned, helmet and boots to be purchased, care, and maintenance. The answer was "yes," if those requirements were met. David was overjoyed, even though he knew it might take several years to truly "earn" his motorcycle by acquiring the agreed upon skills and funds. His parents were thoroughly tested through this episode, but they stuck by their word. David is almost eighteen years old now. He never has had a motorcycle, and he was never told "no." Maybe he'll get one this year, who knows? One thing is for sure, David did a lot of thinking about motorcyles, and if he gets one now it will be a more mature decision than if he had just been told "no" a decade ago.

Opening up the world to your youngsters will surely lessen the frustrations of too many "no's" for kids and parents alike. The more adorable side of your child's spontaneity will shine in an environment of open opportunities and earnable outcomes. There will be a lower chance of "no's" followed by those nasty disputes that mar family harmony. Family Meetings make acquiring self-discipline relatively fun rather than a distressful ordeal.

Safety and Maintenance

Childhood seems inherently fraught with matters of safety and maintenance. "Don't run out in the street!" "Did you brush your teeth?" "Did you check to be sure the heater is off?" "Where are your shoes?" "Who let the cat on the waterbed?" "Do you have your lunch money?" "What time will you be back?" "Is that raspberry jam on your dress?" "Who put the grass clippers in the dishwasher?" It's enough to drive a family nuts. By making safety and maintenance early topics of your Family Meetings you can efficiently prepare your children for life in a world of hazardous products of high technology.

Many safety issues can be made into family games. Have a home fire drill. Simulate escaping from a smoke-filled room with everyone crawling low to the floor to the nearest exit. After a Family Meeting, have a family excursion to check out safety and maintenance features of your house. Where is your smoke alarm? Your fire extinguisher? Your garden hose? Your lantern? Your set of emergency phone numbers? With a positive tone, practice those emergency procedures that make sense in your area. Are there safe places to go in case of storms, floods, or earthquakes? Have you stored water, food, and medical supplies for two or more weeks in case of an earthquake or nuclear disaster? How do things work around the house? Does everyone know enough about electric appliances, circuit breakers, chimney sweeping, slippery tubs, toxins, first aid, and how to stop the toilet from running?

Family Meetings can become preoccupied with mundane issues and details. There is so much on the mechanical level to be learned in childhood. Don't let the material demands of living eclipse the joys of family life. The fact that Family Meetings are effective in handling money and other items of the material world should not preclude your Family Meetings from providing emotional, mental, and spiritual nourishment as well. The very fact that Family Meetings are efficient on the practical level should free you and your family to spend other hours of the days and weeks in even more productive and enjoyable endeavors.

Rewards and Consequences

Money has often served as a reward in the Family Meetings presented here. You can leave money, as such, out of your program completely if you choose. Cold cash or any other supposed reinforcement will only work if it really rewards the child. Money is useful when kids understand its value and when they have made reasonable agreements about its use. For instance, in the Family Notebook section, Gayle, Bill, Daniel, and Michael had worked out in past meetings an understanding about how money could be spent. By agreement, part of Daniel's and Michael's weekly earnings went via Mom to a savings account. The money that remained could be spent mostly at the boy's whim, or with parental permission. More important than the money itself were the good feelings that went along with earning it.

The immediacy of reward is especially important with younger children. Delay of praise or punishment diminishes its effect with little ones. As children get older and can understand the *meaning* of reward and punishment, delays don't matter so much. In the Family Notebook section, nine-year-old Michael accepted doing the laundry as a consequence for yelling and hitting. Although there is little or no connection between aggression and doing the clothes, it worked as a consequence because it was understood as such. Doing the laundry was a meaningful consequence because the family gave it meaning. Michael knew that the effort of doing the wash was intended to remind and motivate him to seek non-violent solutions to his disagreements with his brother.

Corporal Punishment

I have both sympathy and empathy for parents who spank their children or who were themselves whipped as children. Those who practice and believe in physical punishment seem often to hold deep misgivings. Some parents say whippings are harder on them, more energy draining, than for the kids. Others report from experience that spankings lose their effect as the kids get bigger. "With our eleven-year-old spankings don't seem to faze him anymore." What do you do when you spank your child and the bad behavior doesn't go away, or it gets worse? Do you just spank harder? If you have relied on the belt for ten years and it begins to fail, what do you use during the teens?

It should be clear by now that the types of punishment or consequences you use are a personal and private matter to be handled within the sanctity of your own Family Meetings. I have conducted Family Meetings where even the children agreed to spankings as consequences, and also meetings where by agreement spanking or physical punishment was never used. The important point here is that spankings are not necessary. Referring back to the story of Secret Fire: did you notice that little Wesley was not turned over Mom's knee for a spanking? In fact he was never punished or even accused of disobedience for playing with fire. Instead, the problem was *solved*. Had he been spanked, he might have become defensive and armored against learning a better way. As it was, he remained open to changing his behavior rather than becoming stuck in resentment or a lie or worse. If a parent enjoys the retaliation of punishment more than he enjoys a learned change in his child's behavior, that parent should be aware of the price he pays for his conduct. To advertise and glamorize whippings or punishment with no problem-solving is to invite a repetition of the crime. Is it worth the price? Why not solve the problem and skip the whipping?

The unpleasantness of corporal punishment along with its limitations persuades most families that Family Meetings are a far more pleasant and powerful ally than spankings. Families do actually exist which have successfully gone for years, through childhood and all of adolescence, without the need for any physical punishment whatsoever. Regular Family Meetings and a loving home life can make zero corporal punishment *and* good discipline an attainable reality. ***In Family Meetings it is possible to spare the rod but not the discipline.***

Families will discover a great challenge in searching for non-corporal consequences with practical utility and the possibility of being meaningful to a child. It is important that consequences be viewed as an opportunity to learn, and to retain a sense of dignity while doing so. Have you ever sent a child to her room for being bad? There are many ways of doing this. It can be a selfish parental power-play, a conditioned reaction from your own childhood, or a thoughtful and caring service to the future of your child. Sometimes a child is sent to her room for misconduct. The literal words spoken by a parent may be, "Go to your room until I say you can come out." There may be a covert message, ". . .and while you are in your room, you are to feel bad, be miserable as punishment for being bad." In this way the parent may have let off some steam, but what will the child do during her hour of confinement? The youngster will not very likely solve problems and will more likely harbor ill feelings, fear, hate, or resentment of supposed unfairness. If being isolated is to serve as a consequence, it helps greatly to structure the child's time so she'll have something to do with her mind during isolation. Give her a specific mental task to perform so she can earn her way through the consequence. "Go to your room and think a good thought" can serve as a valuable solvent for most minor problems.

Thinking Good Thoughts

If your child doesn't know how to think a good thought, it's not going to work very well to request this as a consequence. Before ever using this technique, prepare your children for its use. You can do this by making a game of thinking good thoughts. First ask your kids what they think "good thought" means. Can they give you an example? You might assist them by giving your own definition. Help your kids recall some happy moments in recent times, playing with Joey, riding horseback, caring for the ducks, rubbing Dad's sore foot. The content doesn't matter so much as the attitude. "Good thoughts" are memories or ideas that are associated with love and happy feelings. As something to occupy a child's mind when sent to his room, good thoughts should be memories of real experiences or positive solutions to problems. Practice good thoughts at a Family Meeting until the youngsters get the hang of it. In this way, a youngster who goes to his or her room to think a good thought bypasses the connotation of having to "think a good thought" as punishment.

At some point you might play a game in which each of the children run to a separate hiding place and quick as can be they each try to think of the best good thought they can. As soon as a youngster thinks of a good thought they are to return to the Family Meeting and share their thought. If acceptable the child might be given a small reward. A snack often works. Then the child runs back to another hiding place to be alone a couple of moments while thinking of another good thought. It can be a competitive game with a prize awarded to the child who thinks the most good thoughts in a certain amount of time. To make it more fair for the younger or inexperienced children, you can make the requirements for the older children stiffer.

Once thinking good thoughts has become positively associated for the children, you might seek family agreement about making good thoughts a component of certain consequences. For example, Joan had two young girls, Shirley (age six) and Kimmy (age five). First, Joan established the play of thinking up a good thought with the girls. Later she used the procedure often when the girls disobeyed or caused too much of a disturbance. Some days were like a merry-go-round. Shirley and Kim would start arguing or picking at each other. Joan would send one to one room and one to another to think good thoughts. The girls didn't have to stay in their rooms any certain length of time, just long enough to think one good thought. As soon as one of the girls got her thought, she'd come racing out to see if Mommy would accept it. Joan would listen for an upward change of mood in the girl's voice. The content of a thought didn't matter much as long as the feeling tone was improved. If Kimmy said, "My good thought is that I will be nice to my sister," that was fine, as long as her attitude had inched up in altitude. If Kim shared a thought that she believed was "good" but she said it in a snippy way, Mom would send her back to her room to try again. Sometimes the girls would succeed at coming up with an acceptable thought and go back to their play, only to start jabbing at each other again. Mom just kept to the rule and kept sending them back for more good thoughts. Don't give up. This technique can work wonders.

Parent Roles

Along with loving and serving your children, in Family Meetings your role is to effect a transfer of your authority to the family as a whole. This transition will be easier if, all during early childhood, you have been wisely and gradually liberating your children. Are they learning more from their own choices and mistakes? Are your youngsters making their own decisions and learning from the consequences? With Family Meetings there is a transformation of a parent's role from being in total charge of your young child to being a team member; you surrender more and more decision-making power to the child. As a youngster grows in the capacity for independence of will-action, as he or she develops a real ability to make moral choices, the more that child has a right to have a "say" in his or her own destiny. The trick is in timing the steps of emancipation for your kids. Not too fast, the little ones might stumble if flooded with liberties too soon. Not too slow, lest the child remain too dependent and too "childish" to grow in the dignity of free will.

If you have become too attached to your child's dependence on you, it may be harder to relinquish this to the group decisions of Family Meetings. Take your time. Time is on your side. Trust the process. Whatever you may feel you are giving up by allowing your kids to grow up and out of affectionate dependency on you, you will be more than amply repaid as you reap the bounty of the discipline of Family Meetings. The discipline of Family Meetings is not the discipline that stifles children into narrow conformity, that dampens their eagerness to explore life. The rigor of Family Meetings need never shut down your child's curiosity nor crush her creativity. ***The discipline of consensual family decisions is the gentle hand of team supervision opening the world for children to have greater and more opportunities for spontaneous delight.*** The discipline of Family Meetings is voluntary, freeing, and uplifting. Ideally, children become more adultlike in terms of moral responsibility and long range thinking while retaining childlike innocence and a child's gleeful spirit.

Family Meetings can assist parents to become more flexible, to recapture a sense of childlike wonder, to identify more fully with the culture of children. Not for a minute do you give up your parental responsibilities in consensual Family Meetings or at any other time. You can sincerely and genuinely enact the role of equal in voting power but you are *always* the parent. Both parents and children can become "childlike" without being "childish." Your role in Family Meetings may be as leader and facilitator, never as owner or boss. There is no reason why you shouldn't make suggestions, and lots of them, in Family Meetings. Feel free to guide the meeting overtly and covertly so long as you abide by the two cardinal Family Meeting rules. It's a wonderful feeling to have your children respect you voluntarily, out of love and not out of fear. This is part of the bounty of turning over personal sovereignty to family sovereignty.

Don't let Family Meetings become a trivial game where the agenda contains only "safe" topics that don't really touch the substance of your children's existence. It's usually a disaster to go only halfway with Family Meetings. If either parent overturns family decisions on his or her own authority, whether by intent or by accident, the best thing to do is to bring the matter before the whole family. Be open to your children's feedback. Are you willing to humble yourself before your children and make amends? They will respect your willingness to be human, and when they see your loyalty to the Family Meeting process they are likely to be permanently impressed. Parental roles that have been established over years will not disappear overnight. If you pull rank against family policy don't ignore it or let pride get in your way. Bring it back to the meeting and acknowledge your slip-up. Solve the problem. Be big enough to take a consequence if it's the consensus. Perhaps there was a reason for your pulling rank, an issue that needs a family policy. If you want the right to take the car keys away from your sixteen-year-old at your discretion, first seek this power directly in a Family Meeting before you usurp that prerogative on your own authority. It's surprising how reasonable and cooperative families can be when the *reasons* for parents' actions and roles are openly discussed and understood. It is true Family Meetings will change you from parent ruler to parent peer, from parent owner to parent partner, from parent mother to parent sister, from parent father to parent brother and from parent force to parent friend. And your children will soar to new altitudes of attitude.

"Goofus" Time

Sometimes with younger children, silliness just takes over a Family Meeting. You'll know intuitively when it's better to surrender and devote a whole meeting to "Goofus" Time. Structured craziness will help relieve the tension of thinking about responsibilities and consequences. Join your children in a giggle contest or "mirth off." Let the topic for the meeting be sheer fun and play. Use props, balloons, crêpe paper, ribbon, drums, old clothes. Be imaginative. Put on a funny costume and surprise your kids. Take the risk of appearing foolish. Have a camera and flash nearby for some truly candid photos. Make each other up with greasepaint or whatever you have. Break out the squirt guns, break the routine. Outlaw seriousness. Play the village idiot in a humorous way. Make faces at each other. Do a somersault. Hold hands in a circle and sing and dance about. Shake, squirm, wiggle, and jiggle. Squeal! Try to sneak up on a mirror. Blither! Blither some more!

With "Goofus" Time you may really be able to turn the table on your kids. Sometimes kids are led to believe that they are the only ones capable of silliness. Show them up. Watch their eyes get big as you do and act in ways they are not used to. Pull the plugs, be creative. Blow the sox off your kids with good humor and a good time. After all, who has had more experience being a kid, you or your child? You, of course. Show your stuff. Later you may be able to use "Goofus" Time as a treat after a regular Family Meeting or as a reward for good conduct. You'll be surprised at how much less silliness interferes with regular family business after your kids see you go "Goofus" a couple of times. When your kids are silly at the the wrong times, you now have a tool. Schedule a "Goofus" period to satisfy everyone's silliness needs. Be careful you don't become addicted yourself, or you may have to take a consequence for being too silly. Once children have experienced "Goofus" Time it will be easier to defer silliness by asking them to agree to wait for the "Goofus" Hour to be silly. It's a safety valve. The kids now have an "out" and are likely to settle more comfortably into the family business. What good would Family Meetings be if you didn't have more time for fun and playful interaction with your children?

Inner and Outer Worlds

A child has both an inner (body-mind), and an outer (worldly-interpersonal) environment to live in and contend with. Each contains a myriad of influences that affect your youngster. In early childhood, the parents, brothers, sisters, and the neighbors have a marked influence on the little ones. Soon school enters into the picture, and by the teens, peers and the media loom high in your son or daughter's milieu. What a world to live in! On the other hand, we would probably all be surprised if we knew just how terribly influential our genetic makeup and body chemistry are in determining our daily behavior—even our thoughts and motives.

Weigh the factors that impinge upon your family. There is a lot to consider: cyclic changes in body chemistry, nutrition, fatigue, stress, weather, social contacts, television, sun spots, and who knows how many other influences? Yet these environmental factors may play heavily into the ease or drudgery of your Family Meetings. Looking back at the Family Meeting notebook of Daniel, Michael, Bill, and Gayle on April 29, there is a note that young Daniel refused to have a Family Meeting. Since there was no consensus, no meeting was held that day. Having the sensitivity to know when to abort a meeting is essential to keep the process working. On the other hand, if you abort too many meetings you will lose the momentum to continue meetings at all. In Bill's family minutes, he states that everyone was cranky from an outing the day before. No need to let a storm of body chemistry defeat the Family Meeting process. But be sure not to let up on having the next meeting at your regular time.

Sometimes a little thought about the environmental factors that press on your children will assist you better to understand their occasionally objectionable conduct. For instance, did you notice from the meeting notes of March 4 that Michael agreed to a consequence for hitting and yelling? Based on the rest of this family's notes, this was pretty strange behavior for usually well-behaved nine-year-old Michael. Notice also, that little Daniel printed at the bottom of the notes, "My brother still sick with cough." Physical illness can so distort the mind that children are just not themselves for a while. In this case, even Michael might not have realized the "extra reason" for his hitting and yelling. Too often children are punished for conduct they don't even understand themselves. Some weeks later another incident with Michael came up involving misconduct with knives. Daniel was in trouble that week for taking candy from his brother. Why were these children misbehaving after so many Family Meetings? It might not be obvious until a broadened perspective of environmental factors comes into view. The

Family Meeting notes don't tell very much, but they do say that the weather was hot. A heat wave can be a real emotional trial for some people. These notes from May 27 are also at the end of the school year, and what parent does not know the ups and downs of those transitions at the beginning and end of a school term? In many places, May 27 would come right at the peak of all those energetic happenings that accompany the end of the spring term. It is difficult to know how much effect these environmental factors had on the boys' conduct, but being sensitive to them does further both empathy and understanding. Whether it is a toddler's irritability that follows eating too much sugar, or the emotional explosion of an adolescent experiencing the hormonal storms of puberty, expand your vision to take into account these sometimes hidden influences. Well-balanced body chemistry, an alert mind, and good cheer are such important ingredients of good Family Meetings that it is worth doing everything you reasonably can to set up the inner and outer environment to support your consensual enterprises.

Sexuality

Most parents feel uncomfortable in dealing with their children's sex education. In a 1977 study nearly seventy percent of all parents admitted trouble in discussing human sexuality with their children. Less than eight percent of these parents ever mentioned contraception to their youngsters, (Katchadourian, 1980, pp.437–439). Fathers are much less likely than mothers to broach the issue of sex. At the same time, these same parents want their kids to have information on sex! They want the schools to take care of it. Presently, sex education is curtailed in public schools. Whatever your values are about sexual conduct and emotions, your kids are going to be exposed to a world of confusion and troubles. Who will integrate in the minds of your children the connections between sexuality, hygiene, love, marriage, child-bearing and family life? Also, abortion, herpes, A.I.D.S., rape, and child pornography are too much a part of our world to be avoided. Isn't it better to educate and prepare our children for the posssible assaults of the world than to default their education to the media and peers?

Family Meetings can provide a perfect structure to discuss sexuality and intimate matters. With younger children, the topic can be taken up naturally in connection with some daily event. Perhaps a neighbor woman is pregnant and your children will be curious to know more about having babies. Even at an early age children have sexual undertones and overtones in their lives. Kinsey reported erection and orgasm in boys only five months old. Evidence for orgasm in girls under the age of three has also been reported. Incest and molestation are more common than you might think. One way or another, your young children are going to be exposed to sexuality. A pet is going to "ride" them, or another youngster is going to engage in "sex play." Even before adolescence, twenty-five percent of young girls in the United States have had sexual contact or have been approached, usually in their own homes by an adult male friend or relative (Katchadourian, 1980, p. 220, 379). Don't your children deserve every opportunity to meet the challenges of their developing sexuality with sound knowledge and good judgment?

If you are just now considering raising the topic of sex education to older children, consider a Family Meeting brainstorm that works like this. You set up your easel and ask any family member to volunteer words that have to do with sex. These can be funny words, formal words, or "dirty" words. Be sure the adults and adolescents volunteer some terms. Write whatever comes up on your easel pad and keep the focus on thinking up more words. This will help diminish the embarrassment associated with any one word. After your brainstorm, check to see if everyone knows the meaning of each term or slang expression. This technique may seem a hard step, but it will desensitize all of your family to using sexual terminology. You can help demystify those four-letter words that carry such big emotional loads for many adults. Children can learn that words are just words—no big deal. If you fear that you don't know enough to answer your kids' questions about sex, refer to a book and share it with your family. The text by Katchadourian (1980) is quite excellent. For young children, Peter Mayle's book, *Where Did I Come From?* is quite good.

Parents have a tremendous influence on their children's gender role development and early perceptions of sexuality. Start at as early an age as language development will permit. If your children don't initiate questions about sex, look for "teachable moments," when there is a natural opening to talk about a sexual topic. For instance, if you are bathing together or if several of you are in the bathroom together, become an "askable parent." Maybe Mom just started her period and this will provide an "askable moment." There is no evidence that any sexual crimes, affective disorders, or other problems come from frank and explicit portrayal of human sexuality. You can teach parental mores to your children with tenderness, understanding, and without suppression. Remember, failure to communicate about sex is itself a communication. Perhaps the kids gather that sexual matters are irrelevant, unimportant, wrong, or embarrassing. If parents in a family setting don't depict sexuality as a natural, beautiful, and gratifying attribute of human nature, who will? Don't let self-consciousness stop you. Go ahead with sex education in your Family Meetings and watch your children become relaxed and well-balanced personalities.

Meditation and Thanksgiving

Family Meetings serve as a fine opportunity to share from your heart, from your essence, the values and deep feelings you hold dear. A simple approach is to take turns and ask each family member to tell about the best happening of the week from his or her point of view. One phrasing of the question might be, "What experience that was true, beautiful, or good happened for you this week?" A similar approach is to have each one go around the table and tell every other family member, individually, one thing that they appreciate about that person. Have these rounds of appreciation with all recipients remaining silent or responding with a simple, "thank you for seeing that part of me."

After everyone has had a turn, allow full expression of what anyone wants to share. These processes can pave the way for a family meditation time.

One way to gather the family energy into a focused Family Meeting is to begin each Family Meeting with a regular ritual of your own creation. Ring a family chime, sing a song, or celebrate your meeting with banners and flowers. For example, begin your meetings by holding hands in a circle at the table. Try to relax and get everyone to take a few really, really deep breaths, "belly breaths." Suggest that everybody close his or her eyes for a moment of silent time. A few minutes of deep quiet can facilitate establishing a level-headed tone at the beginning of your meeting. It gives the little ones a chance to settle down. Your family meditation can be as simple as that, or you can encourage everyone to think quietly about their good "reflections" for the week or year. Everyone has hidden blessings, despite how hard life seems at the moment. Entice your children to search deeply in their minds for their true blessings. What are you really thankful for? What could you shout about? During your meditation time, each of you might share out loud some of your blessings and thoughts of gratitude. These can be cherished moments of family interaction where something seems to emerge that is more and bigger than the sum of your individual contributions. It fills that emptiness inside. Give it a chance!

Assist your children to develop their own values and belief systems based on their own experience. Allow them to trust their own personal experience of living. There's nothing to keep you from making your children aware of your own deep-seated beliefs and convictions. At the same time, your kids will begin to discover meaning and value in your family meditation times. By giving children the freedom to explore their inner world, they are likely to discover truths that you could not give to them even if you wanted to. Your children will be greatly impressed when they see that you are loyal to your values, that you actually endeavor to live by them.

Children are naturally joyful and positive in their outlook. A child's joy can be contagious at family meditation time. Let it be. It's like a breath of fresh air to witness your child begin to discover his or her inner and higher self. Whether you attend a church, a synagogue, a mosque, an ashram, or have no particular practice, Family Meeting meditations can serve to brighten every soul, young and old. Nearly every religion teaches that each person has an inner guide. Whether it is the inner Atman of Hinduism, or the Buddha Nature of Buddhism, or the Ka of the Egyptians, or the Holy Spirit of Christianity, all point to an inner and divine destiny at the core of human nature. Even the "Force" in the *Star Wars* series was an inner force, an inner guide. Luke Skywalker had to listen with an inward ear avoiding anger in favor of a mysterious inner Force. And he eventually succeeded, for even the dark one, Darth Vader, was won over by the Force of love that his own son dared to reveal. Darth Vader lost his life but he was reborn to live on in a higher domain. Family Meetings will encourage your children to see other children as brothers and sisters, common partakers of the inner Mystery—if common partakers, then a common family, the family of humankind, children wanting to share the love and beauty that comes from each family member's inner "heartland."

Scene. At home soon after Family Meeting and quiet time with Mom (*age 36*), Kathy (*age 6*), and Lonnie (*age 11*).

KATHY. Mommy, why do we hold hands at Family Meetings?

MOM. Well, dear, I guess we just like being close to each other, and holding hands is one way of feeling close. What do you think?

KATHY. I like it. It keeps my hands warm and toasty.

MOM. Lonnie, is there some experience you would like to tell about our quiet time?

LONNIE *(closing her eyes for a moment).* I imagined that we were all in a meadow with flowers all around and a waterfall was pouring all around and we were giggling and laughing . . . I don't know, it just felt good.

KATHY. Mommy, . . .

MOM. What, sweetheart?

KATHY. Umm . . . sometimes when we hold hands at Family Meetings, you know when we meditate, I feel goose bumps.

MOM. That's okay dear; does it feel good?

KATHY. Yeah . . . and do you know what else?

MOM. No, what else?

KATHY. Well, yours and Lonnie's hands. . . .

LONNIE. Yeah?

KATHY. Sometimes it feels, . . . it feels like God's hands.

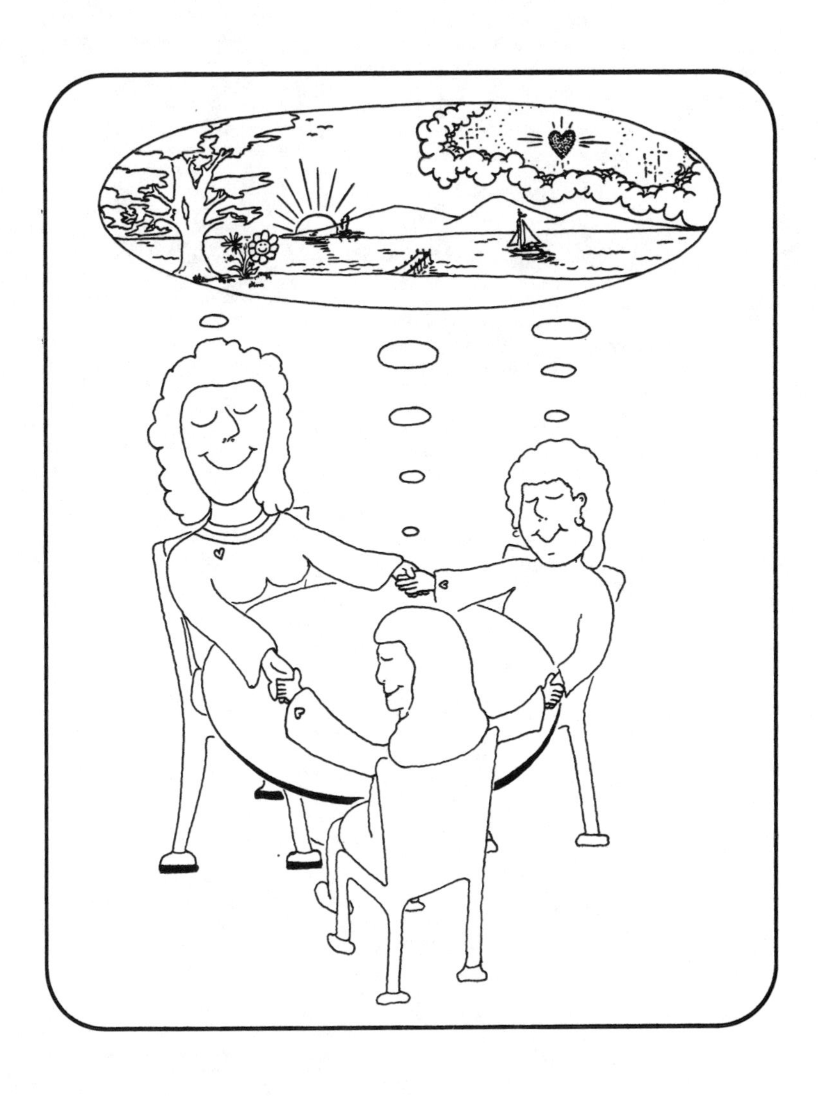

THE TRIUMPH OF LOVE

There is a particularly intriguing aspect to consensual voting. Every single person has absolute power in Family Meetings. What a phenomenon: a democratic representative process of governance where every person's veto is all-powerful. The surprising thing is that with sincere participants, cooperation, and teamwork, love does win out in the long run, at least for families that actually live together and share the reaping of what each other has sown. Even absolute voting power does not inhibit or endlessly bog down the Family Meeting process. In fact, this very voting power enhances mutual love, respect, and self-esteem. Follow the compass of consensual and abiding decisions, and your family will eventually emerge victorious, with its sails full.

How hard it is sometimes, to take the easy way. How insane this world is. We live on a planet with unprecedented material progress, vast natural resources, and records of ages of human experience. The chemistry, the genetics, the computers, the other technologies, and the man-woman-children power are all present on earth now that are capable of changing the world into a beautifully livable and peaceful abode for nearly all of humanity within a few generations. If the ancient Egyptians could span generations to build the pyramids, and if the builders of Stonehenge could span human generations to erect a celestial computer made of monoliths, can't we in the twentieth century span just a few generations with our advanced technologies to ensure a "better country" for our grandchildren's children? Yet, we dawdle on the edge of nuclear cataclysm, more than half the world goes to bed hungry while others groan under the burdens of excess luxury, and millions more live on with affliction and fear. This numbing and nightmarish spectacle can be obliterated by the triumph of love that is born in the humble circumstances of families, the essential building blocks of an enduring civilization.

Take the first small step. If you don't like the brutalization of women and children, toxic chemicals in the environment, the extinction of exquisite animal species, the way the American Indians have been treated, greedy and dishonest politicians, science without ideals, pleasure mania without restraint, the glamorization of crime, dangerous drivers, con artists, terrorists, rapists, and murderers . . . Family Meetings can help.

Choose a positive and aggressive attitude toward Family Meetings and become a welcome member of a network of families that will in fact have a Family Meeting this week. They will make decisions, struggle a bit, share an enjoyable activity, and live trusting that their routine family efforts have meaning and that their aspirations are not in vain, but will be the heritage of generations to come. Surely you will want to make this gift to your family, to the world, and to faith in a future that is worthy of your present labors. Every time you have a Family Meeting, a little more caring is added to the world. Little feet that might have stumbled walk on, more sure-footed in a family's love.

CAN
MY FAMILY LOVES ME.

GAMES AND ACTIVITIES

It is amazing how valuable your local library can be when it comes to finding games and activities for kids (see "Readings and Resources"). The family activities below may prove useful to you in relation to Family Meetings.

Brainstorming

Try having a family brainstorm session about fun activities you all can enjoy together as a family. Set up a chalkboard or an easel, even a large sheet of paper will do, so all your family can see it easily. Ask everyone to "free-associate" about things they like to do as a family. Let the meeting moderator write down each and every idea on the board. Put it up regardless of how irrelevant or silly it seems. After everyone has exhausted their capacity to think up ideas, look over your list and talk about it. If your list of "brainstorm" activities isn't too long, have each family member rate each activity on a ten-point scale where ratings up near ten mean the activity is well-liked while low numbers nearer one mean the activity isn't very popular. Pick one of the items with the highest total rating and agree to do it next week after the Family Meeting.

Videotape a Meeting

Tape record or video a portion of one of your early Family Meetings. Let every family member have equal camera or microphone time. After your meeting, play back the recording and talk about your reactions to seeing yourselves on screen. If your kids have never seen themselves on TV, this can be a thrill. Everyone can gain valuable insights from peeking at themselves in the "time mirror." The needed equipment can usually be rented on an hourly or daily basis at photographic or video stores. Assist your child to see herself in ways she cannot see herself by herself.

Family Exercises

Have a regular family exercise program. Your family workout can be as simple as getting everyone together to do stretches on the living room floor, or you can do yoga, or T'ai Chi, or turn on the music and dance. Encourage your kids to make up their own dances or exercises and teach them to the rest of the family. If you are able to run together or swim or play golf or tennis, all the better.

Gardening

Paradoxical as it may seem soil toil can be very uplifting. Kids can start their own gardens at a very early age. What a great way to learn patience and responsibility and how to care for plants. If you don't have space near your dwelling for a garden plot, kids can grow vegetables in a flower pot on the window sill. The kids will be glad when they get to eat their own vegetables. A similar project is for each family member to sprout some seeds. At the store, pick up some raw corn, peas, alfalfa and bean seeds. Citrus seeds work well, too. Label the seeds in separate containers and let them soak in water overnight. Pour the water off and rinse them daily with fresh water, pouring the water off after each daily rinse. Maybe your kids will want to keep notes or even pictures of their sprouting seeds. The kids can try tasting them at various stages after the seed coat breaks open to see at what point after sprouting the taste is best. This is a fun experiment where kids learn about the process of growing life. They wind up with sprouts to munch on as a healthy treat, to boot.

Cooking

Kids love to cook if given half a chance. Cooking can be a natural extension of gardening or growing sprouts. Imagine eating a meal that your kids have grown and cooked themselves. There are a number of books available now to show kids how to prepare food. For example, *Kids are Natural Cooks*, by Parent's Nursery School, contains child-tested recipes. Knowing how to cook is a basic skill that will stand both boys and girls in good stead as they grow up.

Tell a Dream

You might start or end a Family Meeting by inviting each person to share a dream they have had recently. Have the dreamer tell what she thinks about her dream and why she picked it to share. If she doesn't remember her dreams, she can keep a dream journal or notepad by the bed. As soon as she wakes up after a dream, the youngster can write a note to help recall the dream the next day. Anyone in the family may wish to keep a more elaborate dream journal with daily entries about other daily activities as well. Sometimes, if a dream was scary or confusing, suggest that the dreamer imagine becoming each person and thing dreamed. One at a time, the dreamer tells what it would be like to be, for instance, the monster or the snake or the flower or the angel. Sometimes simple suggestions will enable a child to program her own dreams in ways she chooses. She may even be able to solve problems during dream time. Don't worry about making too much of dream content; it's likely to be just as confusing as it is enlightening. This activity should be light-hearted, and not a ploy for taking yourself too seriously.

Reflection

Reflection is simply thinking back on the past, reviewing a recent day or distant memories. The idea is to generate good thoughts, real memories of happy and positive experiences. As a group, the family can brainstorm some past shared activity that was especially grand. Once you have the topic, like last week's trip to the planetarium, ask each person to recall and tell one fun aspect of the trip. After a child offers his or her fun memory, ask for a deeper look. "Daniel, what was it that made watching the laser show so enjoyable to you?" In this way, assist your child to discover what the ingredients of happiness are. Besides group reflection times, it is a powerful habit to establish a daily quiet time in which each family member thinks back over the day, solving snags or problems, but most of all looking for good memories of happy occasions.

Being in Another's Shoes

This game has to do with empathy, sensing and feeling another person's point of view. First talk to your children. Ask them to tell what they think it would be like to be someone else. Specify who the someone is. What makes it easy to understand another person's point of view (e.g., common language and the fact that we are all human creatures)? What makes it difficult to empathize with another person (e.g., you can't crawl inside their mind and look out)? Once everyone has had a chance to talk about empathy, place a lit candle on the table for atmosphere and lower the illumination in the room. Have everyone hold hands around the candle. Spend a couple of minutes imagining what it would be like being the person holding your right hand. Next, have everyone take off their shoes and place them neatly in a circle in the middle of the floor with the candle safely in the center. Have everyone stand behind their pair of shoes then take a step to the right so everyone is standing behind someone else's shoes. While maintaining a serious attitude have each person put on (as nearly as possible) the next person's shoes. Do this quietly without any talking and just ask everyone to try to feel what it is like to be that person whose shoes they are wearing. After you have traded as many shoes as you wish, sit back down and have each person tell what they experienced. This can be a truly impressive family ritual if you achieve a touch of solemnity.

The Truth Bell Game

This is a game you can play at some of those difficult moments when you can't seem to get agreement about some important matter in your Family Meeting. Suppose your family is stuck with a "yes" or "no" question, for instance, should six-year-old Kathy be permitted to go away with her friend's family for the weekend? First, write down the considerations of each family member. Dad says, "We don't know that family very well." Kathy says, "I want to go more than anything in the world." Her older sister, Madalyne, says, "Kathy, I think you're too crazy about this new friend to be spending a weekend with her so soon." Mom says, "Let's hold hands and play the Truth Bell game."

In this process each person should have the question very clearly in mind. Next everyone holds hands in a circle, closes his eyes, and consults his inner truth indicator. Any question should be viewed in the light of what is truly best for the family as a whole, not just one person. Another way of thinking about this is that you are consulting your better judgement, your intuition, or your deepest subjective sense of what is right. After a couple of minutes of closed-eye inner searching, you can ask, "Did anybody have their truth bells ring?" One or more of your family members may now have a better sense of their choice or more confidence in what they think is right. The younger children or all of you might be given a small bell which can be rung if anyone gets a strong impression that they have discovered some "truth" about the issue at hand.

It takes practice learning to tune into your intuitive "truth bells," so don't give up; keep carrying out the ritual even though it doesn't bear fruit right away. After a while, your family will become skilled at sensing the soundless ring, the inner rush of feeling that something is really right and should be acted on. "Truth bells" work best for value judgements rather than material facts. After a few minutes of silent inner searching, this family talked some more and finally agreed that Kathy should get to know her new friend more before going away with her for the weekend.

Clay Play

If tensions have been running high in your family so that some unwinding recreation is needed, clay can make your day. Check your yellow pages for pottery and stoneware supplies. If you can find out where local potters buy clay for throwing, you will probably be able to buy fifty pounds for a few dollars. Be aware that such clay may stain clothes permanently. It should be kept airtight when not in use! This type of clay is very enjoyable to work with for folks of all ages. Clay objects can be made by molding the clay by hand, or by rolling long "fingers" of clay which then can be coiled into pots, or fences, or forts. This type of clay can be air dried which remains fragile "greenware" or kiln fired to great hardness.

One game to play is to have your family pair up in dyads. Break off a good hunk of clay and place it between each set of partners. Use a clock or stopwatch. Let each partner have two minutes to mold the clay anyway he or she wants, then call time and let the other partner model the same chunk of clay for just two minutes. Let this be a non-verbal or silent activity so neither partner knows what the other is trying to mold. After you have switched partners for a couple of two-to-three-minute sessions, stop the process and talk about how the partners interacted. Did Dad and Kathy compliment each other or cooperate in modeling? Did they compete? Did Dad know that Kathy was trying to make a "gingerbread girl" when time was up and he went on to make the clay into a shoe?

Dyad Mirroring

Another game you can play while still at the Family Meeting table also involves paired partners. Have each family member pick a partner then sit or stand across from each other so that partners are face to face in height. Small kids may need to stand on a box or a chair. Have partners stand or sit facing each other with eyes closed. One of each of the pairs should volunteer as leader of that pair. She begins by slowly opening her eyes while her partner tries to follow or "mirror" her every facial expression and body movement. Take turns being leader while the other partner becomes like a mirror. This game provides some real intimacy and usually triggers much giggling and laughter.

Simon Says

Partner mirroring can extend right on into an old fashioned game of "Simon Says." This is a good game in relation to Family Meetings because all players are equal in status during the game except for the leader, and you can take turns being leader. Kids learn quickly to listen carefully and discriminate among verbal messages. If Mom is the leader, and she says, "Simon says, touch your toes," everyone should touch their toes, but if Mom says, "touch your nose," then no one should move. If you don't say, "Simon Says," then no one should do anything. If they move, they are "out" of the game for now. In this game, even Kathy gets to tell Dad what to do. Everyone gets to learn to give and take directions cheerfully. You can also work this game into a discussion of morals by asking, "should you do anything Simon says?"

Magic Paste

"Magic Paste" is a bit messy but can be made in the house for kids of all ages to experiment with. Pour a box of powdered corn starch into a large flat cake pan that is about two inches deep. Add tap water little by little and have the kids stir this concoction until about a quart of water is added. When the paste sits on the cake pan there may be a thin film of water on top. Now ask your family what would happen if you suddenly slapped this goo full force with your open hand. Will the paste splatter all over? Try it. What happens when you slap the magic paste? Your kids will probably enjoy exploring other properties of this carbohydrate concoction. It's messy but it sure can be fun!

Home Dough

It's not made with corn starch but you can do it at home. Make your own family money. The kids can have great fun designing the paper bills, cutting coins out of cardboard, and deciding on the denominations. If rewarding your kids with cash via Family Meetings doesn't appeal to you, perhaps "home dough" can be an alternative. Family money can be issued by any family member as a promissory note. As an illustration, Dad signed his name to a paper "dollar" Kathy made that was redeemable for one game of checkers. Mom signed a bill that was a promise to take a family member for one ride in the car. Any youngster who earned this token could redeem it for a ride to the store or school. A whole banking and monetary system can be developed right in your own household. The kids learn a ton from making and earning "home dough."

Sneaking up on a Mirror

This is a silly sport but it can be a wonderful diversion for kids of all ages. As parent you may want to demonstrate the proper technique. First you tell the family which mirror you are going to sneak up on. It's best to sneak up on a mirror that is affixed to a wall or door so the mirror doesn't move while you are sneaking up on it. Don't let the mirror know you are sneaking up on it. First walk around casually so no mirrors suspect you are sneaking up on them. If your reflection appears in the mirror at any time while you are sneaking around, you're caught! Be very slow and stealthly. Creep and crawl across carpets, inching your way toward the unsuspecting mirror. Gradually inch up the wall next to the mirror being very quiet with every move. Once you are very close to the mirror, at just the right moment jump in front of the mirror and see if you can see it before it can see you. Will you ever win? Pretty silly, but little kids love it. You may be able to turn this game into an interesting discussion of the physics of light and optics. How fast does light travel? Perhaps you will discuss the phenomenon of reflectivity.

Star Gazing

A simple activity on a clear night is for the family to go outside, lie down and look up at the heavens. See how many planets and other celestial objects you can identify. At the proper seasons you will be able to see the moon, the big dipper, the little dipper, and perhaps the Milky Way. The seemingly brightest stars are really the planets Jupiter, Venus and Saturn. Do your children know about galaxies and the fact that the Milky Way is a huge galaxy, tens of thousands of light years across. Is our planet Earth a part of the Milky Way? If you imagine passing a straight line through the two stars forming the outer side of the big dipper, the part of that line that goes up north will just about run into the North Star, Polaris. This star is important because it appears to be fixed in the heavens year around while all the other celestial bodies seem to move season by season. Why is that? How would you use the North star for navigation? What is a shooting star?

Compose a Family Letter

Is there a relative or friend to whom you haven't written for a long time? A fun way to write a composite letter is to start with Dear Grandma, then have each person take turns in contributing just one or so words. Kathy might say "We," then it would be her sister's turn. Maybe she says, "miss," and mom says, "you." Each successive person trys to keep making sense by adding a word to those already said. Your letter may not be long but writing it can be a bundle of laughs.

Animals

Everyone knows about animals but it seems worthwhile emphasizing how much fun and serviceable a pet or pets can be for kids. Children often learn early habits of affection from and for pets. Caring for a helpless creature is a natural way to bring out the more tender and affectionate sides of your youngsters. Even without a pet, kids can learn much from watching animals in nature. Is there a bird sanctuary or other game preserve near you? Here's a great opportunity for a family outing.

A Puppet Family

Just by painting the toe end of a white sock or by wrapping a balloon with papier mâché your youngsters can create a puppet face. Have each family member make a puppet of another family member. A child would make a puppet to represent his brother or sister, or everyone can fashion their own puppet. Now, have a puppet show, first with everyone using the puppet that represents themselves. You can re-enact a past fun experience you have had as a family. Next, enact some type of drama you make up but exchange puppets so each person gets to "speak" as though he were Sis, or Dad, or Mom. Many intriguing conversations can be had with puppets as vehicles for intimacy. See what comes up for you. (See Hunt, 1982).

Some of these games will get you started with some rewards for your Family Meeting business. There is a lot of entertainment in the world for children and much less that is really meaningful. It's not so much what you do as a family, but the way in which you do it. Pick a way with heart and you'll have a good time no matter how lame the game may be. Just in case you need a few more ideas: Where is the nearest genuine locomotive ride you can treat your children to? Have you been camping lately? Is there an opportunity in your area to go ice skating or snow skiing? How about wind surfing? For an indoor game, are you familiar with "Hoosker-Du" from Holland? It's an intriguing board game for kids six to twelve. Do you save crumbs to feed to the ducks at the lake? Is there a government fishery near you? These facilities often have huge tanks of fishes of every size. Sometimes you can buy food from a coin dispenser and watch the fish all swarm up to a few flakes of chow. Riddles, puzzles, mazes and masks can all be made at home with paper and pencil. Singing with the kids or playing musical instruments can be super. If a little one starts to stutter, assist him to sing his messages and watch his stuttering get better. There are always math games and arithmetic puzzles. For instance, take a piece of paper and make three straight rows and columns of three dots each. Can you connect all the dots with only four straight lines and without lifting your pencil? Have you played ping pong, pool, croquet or miniature golf with your kids lately? Best of all, have you made it a point to show another family how to have Family Meetings?

LOVE
FAMILY MEETINGS

READINGS AND RESOURCES

Altas, Stephen L. *Parents without Partners Sourcebook.* Philadelphia: Running Press, 1984.

This is a reassuring reference and guide for any single parent. The author surveys the whole gamut of issues facing single mothers and fathers. Special attention is given to custody and alternatives to custody, to single parent finances, as well as discipline, outside resources, visitation, church, remarriage, divorce, step-parenting, the military, and how to enjoy being single. This book is an offshoot of the Parents without Partners organization, 7910 Woodmont Avenue, Bethesda, MD 20814 (192 pgs., paper).

Auerbach, Stevanne. *The Whole Child: A Sourcebook.* New York: Perigee (Putnam) Books, 1981.

Dr. Auerbach provides a rich resource book on child-rearing from babyhood to older childhood. She takes up about one hundred topics related to parenting and sets them forth in alphabetical order. For many topics she gives tips and information, annotated bibliographies, checklists, games and projects, self-tests, films and audiovisual aids, and where to go for more information. Some of her intriguing topics include: "Drugs, Diet, X-Rays and Illness," "Infant Care," "Baby-Sitters," "Drama," "Gifted Children," "Kisses," "Moral Development and Values," "Religion," "Rights of Children," "Sexual Equality," and "Single Parents." She also provides appendices with resources in terms of organizations, toy manufacturers, books, and museums. This is a valuable and comprehensive book for parents at any stage of parenting (304 pgs., paper, photo illustrations).

Bell, Ruth and Wildflower, Leni Z. *Talking with Your Teenager: A Book for Parents.* New York: Random House, 1983.

This is a resource work that gives anecdotes, advice, answers to questions, and example dialogues of teen-parent interactions about a variety of issues. The authors take up first, "Our own issues," then move on to cover the changes of puberty, communication, various teen problems, emotional health, sex, drugs, and even eating disorders (126 pgs., paper, photo illustrations).

Boston Children's Medical Center and Gregg, Elizabeth M. *What to Do When There's Nothing to Do: 601 Tested Play Ideas for Young Children.* New York: Dell, 1968.

This is a time-tested source of ideas to facilitate good interactions and good play for your young children. This book is structured by age groups, young to older. It is filled with a host of ideas: cooking, cleaning, books, records, and more (186 pgs., paper, illustrations).

Bramnick, Lea and Simon, Anita. *The Parents' Solution Book: Your Child from Five to Twelve.* New York: Perigee, 1984.

Although Family Meetings are not a topic of this book, the authors have organized their headings according to practical daily activities that children are bound to participate in. The authors' ideas can easily be transferred to the Family Meeting situation. Under "Everyday Activities," the authors discuss "Planning Prevents Problems," "Mornings," "After School," "Alone Time," and "Bedtime." Under "Quality Time," they cover items such as, "Sports," "Shopping," "Cooking," "TV," and "Travel." Under "Health and Safety," doctor visits, immunization, and preparing children to see various health providers. Their last chapter, "Responsibilities and the Maturing Child," deals with "Self-image," "Sex Role Identification," "Pets," and "Sleepovers." In a section called "Promoting High Achievement," a Chicago research study has shown that it is perseverance, not high IQ that predicts high achievement in youngsters (334 pgs., paper, lightly illustrated).

Colao, Flora and Hosansky, Tamar. *Your Child Should Know: Protect Your Children from Assault and Crime.* New York: Berkeley Books, 1985.

"The sex offender will keep trying until he finds a child who has not been given this training." This is the theme of a book that deals with a difficult topic to face: sexual abuse of children. The authors intend to assist you to train your child in self-defense and techniques to prevent assault, abduction, and abuse. Their book ends with a piercing chapter, "What to do if it happens . . . a step by step guide" (179 pgs., paper).

Dinkmeyer, Don and McKay, Gary D. *The Parent's Handbook, STEP: Systematic Training for Effective Parenting.* Circle Pines, Minnesota: American Guidance Service, 1982.

The theme of this book is democratic and positive parenting. It follows the P.E.T. system and acknowledges that effective parents are not born; they must learn specific skills. The authors include many practical examples, charts, and illustrations. The authors actively engage the reader in goal-setting, problem-solving, and communication skills with written exercises and other projects. They include a chapter on natural and logical consequences and an excellent brief chapter on Family Meetings. They discuss guidelines for Family Meetings, leadership skills, how and when to begin meetings, and list six common mistakes in Family Meetings: 1) waiting too long for everyone to attend, 2) starting late, 3) meeting for too long a time, 4) domination by one or more persons, 5) overemphasis on complaints and criticisms, 6) not putting agreements into actions (120 pgs., paper, color illustrations).

Dinkmeyer, Don and McKay, Gary D. *The Parent's Guide: The STEP Approach to Parenting Your Teenager.* Circle Pines, Minnesota: American Guidance Service, 1983.

This is similar to the book mentioned above except that this volume is devoted solely to teenagers. Topics include: understanding teenagers, personality development, emotions, self-esteem, listening, communication, expressing, discipline, Family Meetings, and special challenges of the teens. They take up some of the special issues regarding Family Meetings with teenagers. "What can be done about broken agreements?" "What if my teenager won't participate?" The authors give an example of a Family Meeting dialogue regarding a youngster's messiness. Emphasis is placed on reflective listening and giving feedback through "I messages" (192 pgs., paper, illustrations).

Dodson, Fitzhugh. *How to Father.* New York: Signet, 1975.

Dr. Dodson has written a number of books: *How to Parent,* 1970; *How to Discipline with Love,* 1978; *How to Grandparent,* 1981. *How to Father* is an inexpensive and excellent paperback that takes a thorough and loving, developmental approach to childrearing. The first chapters are a guide to fathering through each stage of childhood, followed by an important chapter on divorced parents. There is a wealth of resources in his appendices: toys, play, books, records, and a survival kit for fathers (497 pgs., paper, lightly illustrated).

Dow, Emily, R. *Now What Shall We Do?* New York: M. Barrows and Company, 1966.

This book is subtitled "The family book of things to do and games to play." Activities are organized by interesting topics like special days, summer activities, rainy and stay-in-bed days, and what to do on Valentine's Day, birthdays, the Fourth of July, and Easter. The author includes car games like Twenty Questions, and "How Many?" games like, "How many words can you think of that are pronounced the same but are spelt differently?" Puzzles to play alone, carpentry, costumes, and weather finish off her list (273 pgs., cloth, illustrated).

Dreikurs, Rudolf. *Children: the Challenge.* New York: Hawthorn/Dutton, 1964.

The author is a psychiatrist of the Adlerian persuasion. He urges parents to be neither permissive nor punitive. His book is filled with specific examples of issues with kids, how parents usually handle the situations, and then a detailed explanation of how to better handle each situation with Adlerian principles. Dreikurs has a chapter on natural and logical consequences (p.76), and a chapter on Family Councils (p.301). He underscores the importance of a young child's feelings of security and how he or she depends on a feeling of belonging (p.14). He distinguishes the business of the child from that of the parent. For example, "let" Alice eat on her own, that's her business, don't coax her (p.78). On page 84 he states, "We must realize that we no longer live in an autocratic society that can 'control' children but in a democratic society that needs to 'guide' them. We can no longer impose our will on our children." Dreikurs has written a series of ten or more books dealing with the challenges of child-training, marriage, parenthood, misbehavior, the classroom, learning, and discipline without tears. *Children: the Challenge* is worth having and will prove complementary to your success with Family Meetings, (335 pgs., paper).

Dreikurs, Rudolf; Gould, Shirley; and Corsini, Raymond. *Family Council: The Dreikurs Technique for putting an end to war between parents and children (and between children and children)*. Chicago: Henry Regnery Company, 1974.

This is a text that deals specifically with Family Council practices. The authors set the stage by discussing topics such as, "Human Beings Can Function Only as Equals," "Logic Works Better than Force," and "Well-Being Depends on Cooperation." Dreikurs emphasizes the German word, *gemeinschaftsgefühl,* a concern for others. His Family Council procedures are rather formal. There are rules and definitions of terms like, "open forum" and "freedom of expression." He includes these chapters: "Explanation of Terms," "Why Have Family Councils?," "Getting Started," "Techniques," "Planning and Procedure," and "Coping with Conflict." Detailed examples of tasks around the house and how to divide up the labor are given in chapters, "Sharing Responsibilities" and "Special Tasks." Two later chapters focus on mistakes and difficulties in carrying out Family Councils. This valuable text on democratic Family Councils is compatible with *A Family Meeting Handbook* (110 pgs., cloth).

Gardner-Loular, JoAnn; Lopez, Bonnie; and Quackenbush, Marcia. *Period.* 330 Ellis Street, #518 Department B, San Francisco, California 94102, 1981.

For girls entering adolescence, this is a simply illustrated book about menstruation. In simple language it covers everything from pubic hair to tampons. The authors discuss important topics such as feelings, having a period at school, pelvic exams, and hormones. There are touching little cartoon vignettes (87 pgs., paper, illustrated).

Gordon, Thomas. *Parent Effectiveness Training.* New York: Peter H. Wyden, 1970.

Gordon presents a system or "method" of childrearing. He is very conscious of child culture and the rights and needs of children. This system uses democratic family council practices, "Method III," and Gordon stresses the involvement of both parents. He feels that they can assist children in their development in many ways. For instance, Gordon says that children have to learn to identify and label their emotions. Parents can contribute directly to this process, but parents may not know these things naturally. They can be trained in one of the many P.E.T. workshops held across the country (300 pgs., paper, illustrated).

Gordon, Thomas. *Parent Effectiveness Training in Action: Inside P.E.T. Families, New Problems, Insights, and Solutions.* New York: Peter H. Wyden, 1976.

This is a continuation of the themes in the earlier book. The title gives an apt description. More information about the P.E.T. programs can be requested at: Effectiveness Training Associates, 110 South Euclid, Pasadena, California, 91101, or phone (213)796-5107.

Gurman, Alan S. and Kniskern, David P. (Eds.) *Handbook of Family Therapy.* New York: Brunner/Mazel, 1981.

This weighty tome applies a medical model toward family life and the problems therein. Lengthy sections cover Family Therapy in the context of history, psychoanalysis, integrational and system theories, behavioral models, and so on. In one section there is a list of principles of healthy families. Included are, "nonpassive warmth," open, honest, and clear communication, outside involvement, and empathy (796 pgs., cloth).

Hearne, Betsy. *Choosing Books for Children: A Common Sense Guide*. New York: Dell Press, 1982.

A list of over one hundred titles are included by some of the best known children's book writers such as Dr. Seuss, Babbitt, and Fox. The author starts with recommendations of books for preschoolers and works her way up to the teens. In the last section, "The Goose is Loose," she provides an interesting discussion of sex, violence, fear, and censorship in children's literature (180 pgs., paper, little illustrations).

Hunt, Robert. "Growing Up with Your Children." Sebastopol, California: Family Relations Foundation, 1985.

Robert Hunt, Ph.D., is Professor of Mathematics at California State University, Humboldt. Dr. Hunt is also the father of thirteen children. His paper on parenting is touchingly profound and powerfully reassuring to all parents. Perhaps this quotation typifies his approach, "You have nothing more precious to offer your child than yourself." Dr. Hunt's article is available from Family Relations Foundation. Refer to the final page of this handbook (24 pgs., paper).

Hunt, Tamara and Renfro, Nancy. *Puppetry in Early Childhood Education*. 1117 West 9th Street, Austin, Texas: Nancy Renfro Studios, 1982.

This is a comprehensive and practical guide for parents and children showing children how to make and use puppets. There is a systematic coverage of puppetry as a process, puppet play, presenting literature and music through puppetry, making puppets, and then a very nice section on dramas kids can enact with their puppets. For example, she describes the procedure used by kids who were planning a puppet show called "Henny Penny." Kids made puppets like Ducky Lucky and Goosey Loosey, then were asked this question, "If a nut fell on your head out of a tree but you didn't know what it was, what would you think?" A description of how to carry out the puppet show follows (258 pgs., paper, detailed how-to illustrations).

Johnson, Eric W. *Love and Sex in Plain Language.* New York: Lippincott, 1977.

This is a good book for your older child or teenager to read in order to learn about sexual matters. It covers the basic cellular, anatomical, and functional facts of human sexuality. Emotional issues regarding VD, masturbation, contraception, rape, incest, and homosexuality are nicely handled. The understanding of terms is emphasized; new words are clearly defined and set apart in boldface type (112 pgs., cloth, illustrations).

Johnson, Spencer. *The One Minute Mother.* New York: William Morrow, 1983.

The One Minute Mother, The One Minute Father, and *The One Minute Manager,* are all brief, readable books that take a few simple, but profound, ideas and present them in an appealing way. Here are some of the principles that Dr. Johnson presents in storybook form: ". . . children who like themselves like to behave themselves . . . you act best when you feel good about yourself . . . we become what we think about." There are three major steps in this book: 1) One Minute Goals where, "I take a minute, I look at my goals, I look at my behavior, I see if my behavior matches my goals." 2) One Minute Praisings where, "I catch my children doing something right." 3) One Minute Reprimands where, I reprimand my children as soon as possible. I am specific and I tell my children how I feel. I touch my children to let them know I am on their side. I signal the end of the reprimand with a hug, "when the reprimand is over—it's over!" (112 pgs., cloth).

Judson, Stephanie. *A Manual on Nonviolence and Children.* Philadelphia: New Society Publishers, 1983.

This book is the outgrowth of a conference held by the Friends' Peace Committee of Philadelphia. Changing tradition, changing competitive games to cooperative games, conflict resolution, and activities are discussed. There is a chapter on meetings that can be directly applied to Family Meetings. The ingredients of a good meeting involve: common goals, clear processes for achieving those goals, awareness that each person comes to the meetings with preoccupations and preconceptions, and a sense of involvement in the meeting. In a section on "Agenda Planning," the essentials are: gathering people together, agenda review, main items, announcements, and evaluation of the meeting. She suggests having a "Vibes Watcher" at your meetings to identify the emotion tones during your meeting. She says about closing your meeting, "Try to end the meeting in the same way it started—with a sense of gathering. Don't let it just fizzle. A song, some silence, standing in a circle, shaking hands—anything that affirms the group. . ." (152 pgs., paper, illustrations).

Katchadourian, H. A., and Lunde, D. T. *Fundamentals of Human Sexuality.* (3rd Ed.) New York: Holt, Rinehart and Winston, 1980.

This is a very readable, comprehensive, and excellent textbook on sexuality. The authors are medical doctors who take a cross-cultural and objective look at sexuality from many perspectives. Did you know, for instance, that nearly a billion people in the People's Republic of China have a very low divorce rate, compared to 40% for new marriages in the U.S.A.? The Chinese limit their families to one or two children, and contraception and abortion are usually free (pp. 484–485). This is a good reference book for your Family Meetings regarding sexuality (534 pgs., paper, illustrated).

Larrick, Nancy. *A Parents' Guide to Children's Reading.* New York: Doubleday, 1975.

This is another good resource for discovering good reading for your children. Nancy Larrick offers over seven hundred annotated titles. She takes a developmental approach and follows chidrens' reading in stages, beginning with the baby, going to "From four to six," "When he starts to school," "As he begins to read," "Independence in the 3rd and 4th grades," "More grown up and more demanding," and then moving on to cover much more, including TV, almanacs, poetry, and using the library (448 pgs., cloth).

Latter-day Saints, Church of Jesus Christ of. *Family Home Evening.* Salt Lake City, Utah, 1976.

This is a beautifully executed handbook designed for believers of the Mormon religion. Although more than half of this book is devoted to the particular teachings and practices of the church, there are a number of chapters that may have more universal appeal. For example, a sample from p. 128, "Learning to Think Good Thoughts," says, "Have each family member decide on something definite he can place in his mind to use when he needs to replace an undesirable thought with a good one." The text goes on to make specific directions. There are also valuable sections on "overcoming feelings of revenge," "meaningful prayer," "going the second mile," "how-to-do-it helps," and more (207 large pgs., paper, color illustrations).

Latter-day Saints, Church of Jesus Christ of. *Family Home Evening Resource Book*. 47 East South Temple Street, Salt Lake City, Utah 84150, 1983.

This is a continuation of resources for the Family Home Evening type of Family Meeting mentioned above. The first half of the book pertains to Mormon religious training. The second half consists of resources for building a strong family. The book contains thirty-seven Family Home Evening lessons on topics including personal integrity, unconditional love—key to effective parenthood, achieving oneness in marriage, reasoning with children, and reclaiming a wayward child. There is a generous supply of family activities including cultural activities, songs, nature activities, and family disaster preparedness (346 pgs., paper, color illustrations).

Lickona, Thomas. *Raising Good Children*. New York: Bantam Books, 1985.

Dr. Lickona, Ph.D., is a developmental psychologist at the State University of New York. His book is a thorough manual on parenting and child development. He places special attention on understanding your children, especially the typical behavior characteristic of different ages. He also has a section on concerns that cross all stages. Some topics are: getting kids to talk to you, fairness, the "ask-don't-tell" method of reasoning, teaching by telling, TV, sex, drugs, and drinking. Two headings on Family Meetings focus on, "How to use the fairness approach in Family Meetings," and "A safe way to begin Family Meetings." The type of meetings suggested by Dr. Lickona are termed, "fairness meetings," and they always involve consensual decision making (446 pgs., paper).

Long, Lynette and Long, Thomas. *The Handbook for Latchkey Children and Their Parents*. New York: Arbor House, 1983.

Concerning any child who must stay home alone while her or his parents work, this book is excellent. Here are some issues that the authors discuss: stress, sibling relations, being alone, fears and dangers, programs that work, and more. Particularly helpful and empathetically written sections deal with "life before school," about kids who are home alone on weekday mornings, and a chapter on "when not to leave a child alone" (316 pgs., paper).

Mayle, Peter. *"Where Did I Come From?"* New Jersey: Lyle Stuart, Inc., 1973.

This is a wonderful little book to use to introduce your small children to sexuality. It's illustrated with comical figures designed to relieve the embarrassment a young reader might feel regarding its rather explicit portrayal of love-making, genitals, conception and pregnancy (50 pgs., cloth, color illustrations).

Mayle, Peter. *"What's Happening to Me?"* New Jersey: Lyle Stuart, Inc., 1979.

This is a continuation of themes from the book above. It claims, "answers to the world's most embarrassing questions." Illustrations are funny, except where anatomy is critical, then there are representational drawings. Mayle covers puberty, erection, bras, voice changes, pimples, wet dreams, masturbation, and circumcision in a charming style (50 pgs., cloth, illustrated in color).

Nelson, Gerald E. *The One Minute Scolding*. Boulder, Colorado: Shambala Books, 1984.

Dr. Nelson, M.D., writes a simple but psychologically oriented book that develops a positive form of scolding children. He deals, for instance, with how conscience develops. There is an interesting section on "spanking," as well (144 pgs., paper).

Nutt, Grady. *Family Time: A Revolutionary Old Idea.* The Million Dollar Round Table, 2340 River Road, DesPlaines, Illinois 60018, 1977.

This book conveys a specialized and somewhat idosyncratic approach to Family Council practices. The family in history is discussed, family communication, a family how-to night, family service projects, family awards, music night, family traditions, decision making, outing times, Boy Scouting, and a section for adults, "Parent to Parent" (84 pgs., paper, color illustrations).

Painter, Genevieve, and Corsini, Raymond. *The Practical Parent: Solutions to the Everyday Problems of Raising Children.* New York: Cornerstone Library, 1984.

Doctors Painter, Ed.D. and Corsini, Ph.D. take a positive approach to child-rearing involving a balance of love and discipline. Their first section deals with "Fundamentals of Practical Parenting," in which they cover issues such as "Natural and Logical Consequences." Next, they take up "Problems of Routine Living," such as dressing, eating, getting up, and keeping clean. In a section on "Interacting," they emphasize positive methods of dealing with "fighting." Under "Special Problems," they cover "Temper Tantrums," "Nightmares," "Bed-wetting," and "Bowel Control." In a final section on "Building Cooperative Families," they have many ideas on inter-family networking. One whole chapter is devoted to "The Family Council." Their Family Meeting philosophy emphasizes that attendance is not required, and that the Family Council must be distinct from family discussions at dinner or in the car. The authors suggest concensus and what they call keeping order by "feet," that is, a person's feet can walk them away from the meeting at any time. The authors state, "Were we to be limited to only one recommendation to help create a happy, cooperative family, we would say, 'Start a Family Council' " (246 pgs., paper).

Parent's Nursery School. *Kids Are Natural Cooks.* Boston: Houghton Mifflin, 1974.

This book is subtitled, "Child-tested recipes for home and school using natural foods." This cook book follows themes like food for certain seasons, for cold days, for holidays, picnics, and cooking for animals. It contains dozens of interesting and unusual recipes suitable for children to create with a little parental supervision. There is a guide for teachers and parents ranging from nutrition to equipment and emotional aspects of eating and cooking (129 pgs., spiral bound, illustrations).

Ricci, Isolina. *Mom's House, Dad's House: Making Shared Custody Work.* New York: Macmillan, 1980.

The author touches on nearly every posssible topic concerning children of divorced parents. Some of her chapters are: "Two Homes with No Fighting," "They Said it Couldn't Be Done," "The View from Where You Stand," "The Map from Home to Home," "Watch Your Language," "Your Human Income," "Emotions at the End of Marriage," "Retreat from Intimacy," "Business," "Legal Business," "The Open Family," "Long-Distance Parenting," and "Reinvolving the Dropout Parent." The author also includes appendices and helpful self-surveys (270 pgs., paper).

Richter, Betts. *Something Special Within.* Box 779, Sonoma, California 95476: Be All Books, Publishers, 1978.

This is a fine little book for ages 3–7. It is warmly written and illustrated with emphasis on love, inner guidance, and happy thoughts. "There is something very special within you, waiting for your joy of discovery" (41 pgs., paper, illustrations).

Rogers, Fred and Head, Barry. *Mister Rogers Talks with Parents.* New York: Berkley Books, 1983.

Mr. Rogers of the *Mister Roger's Neighborhood* TV show tells what he has learned from his years of helping children to grow. Some subjects he discusses are: being there, privacy, disabilities, play, competition, television, going to the doctor (dentist, hospital, hairdresser), moving, death, divorce, family occassions, and alone time. An example of his wisdom on the topic of discipline is, ". . . discipline and punishment are different . . . I now think of discipline as the continual everyday process of helping a child learn *self*-discipline." He writes in a conversational style and recites many personal anecdotes from his own family. There are also seventy pages of musical scores—songs such as, *It's a Beautiful Feeling* and *Good People Sometimes Do Bad Things* (315 pgs., paper, illustrated).

Schaefer, Charles E. *How to Talk to Children about Really Important Things*. New York: Harper & Row, 1984.

Dr. Schaefer is a child psychologist and author of several other books about children. Although Family Meetings are not a content topic of this volume, there are many practical ideas that can be easily adapted to a Family Meeting context. Some of his ideas can even fill the role of answering, "What shall we discuss at our next Family Meeting?" His book is nicely ordered with many easy-to-read topics and answers to questions. Going to the hospital, death, sexual abuse, being adopted, starting school, money, moving to a new home, conception, homosexuality, risks and failures, prejudice, God, war, and drinking are all "important things," according to the author (157 pgs., paper).

Schwartz, Alvin. *How to Fly a Kite, Catch a Fish, Grow a Flower, and Other Activities for You and Your Child*. New York: Macmillan, 1965.

This is a very practical and useful resource. Bikes, skating, athletics (baseball, football, tennis, basketball), water activities, camping, snow sports, hobbies, crafts, kites, cooking, magic, secret codes, nature, seeds, trees, wild plants, gardening, birds, insects, reptiles, mammals, pets, stars, zoos, and museums are all included (208 pgs., cloth, illustrations). There is a paperback version of this topic: *The Rainy Day Book,* Simon and Schuster, 1973.

Stein, Sara Bonnett. *Learn at Home the Sesame Street Way*. New York: Simon and Schuster, 1979.

Learning principles used in the TV show are applied through creative games and activities. The book deals with three types of goals: I. Cognitive, having to do with counting and naming for little ones; II. Affective, having to do with positive self-image and cooperation; III. Physical, having to do with nutrition, hygiene, posture and related matters. There are sections on role-playing and mini-dramas, along with hundreds of educational games and activities ranging from making piñatas to learning sign language (286 pgs., cloth, illustrations.)

Wyckoff, Jerry, and Unell, Barbara C. *Discipline Without Shouting or Spanking*. New York: Meadowbrook Books, 1984.

This is a book primarily aimed for training preschoolers. It is a listing of many practical problems and practical solutions. Although the Family Meeting approach is not discussed, there are many tips and suggestions easily transferable to the Family Meeting procedure. Here is a sampling of ideas these authors take up: resisting going to bed, getting up, not eating, playing with food, tantrums, whining, talking back, aggressive conduct, sibling conflicts, toilet issues, clinging to parents, various ways of being demanding, travel, and more (135 pgs., paper).

TO ORDER *A FAMILY MEETING HANDBOOK:*

North America: Send your check or money order for $7.95 (Canada, $8.95) per copy, plus $1.00 handling and shipping, and 6% ($.48) sales tax for California residents to Family Relations Foundation, (P.O. Box below). Be sure to include *your name, address, the number of copies you want, and your check.* Please allow time for personal checks to clear the bank before your order is shipped.

Other Countries: Orders received from countries outside the continental United States should include an international money order for $8.95 (U.S.), plus $1.00 (U.S.) shipping and handling, and an amount to cover postage. The shipping weight for each copy of the handbook is 10.7 oz. (300 g). Specify whether the postage fee is for air or surface mail.

TO ORDER "Growing Up with Your Children," by Robert Hunt, Ph.D.:

Send your check or money order for $3.00 (Canada, other countries, $4.00) per copy, plus $.50 shipping and handling, and 6% ($.18) sales tax for California residents to Family Relations Foundation, (address below).

TO WRITE TO FAMILY RELATIONS FOUNDATION ABOUT YOUR FAMILY:

If you will enclose a self-addressed stamped envelope with your inquiry or comment, a member of the Family Relations staff will personally reply to your comment or question about Family Meetings. Any person or organization interested in having a seminar or workshop on Family Meetings may inquire about our speaker and workshop services. If you are interested in participating in a Family Meeting parents' network and support group in your area, let us know and we will place you on our mailing list and keep you informed of developments in your area. Send all inquiries and comments to the address listed below.

TO CALL THE FAMILY RELATIONS NETWORK LINE:

If you have questions, comments, anecdotes, or problems with your Family Meetings, the Family Relations Network Line will be open with trained staff available to respond to your phone calls between 4:00 p.m. and 7:00 p.m., Pacific Standard Time, Mondays only, (no collect calls please). Information about Family Meeting networking is available by phone as well as by mail.

(707) 823-0876

Family Relations Foundation is a Nonprofit Public Benefit Corporation dedicated to positive relations among all family members and to the joy and well-being of the family as an institution. Your tax deductible donations are welcomed with gratitude.

Family Relations Foundation
P.O. Box 462
Sebastopol, California 95472, U.S.A.